D1558852

Joyce's Misbelief

The Florida James Joyce Series

UNIVERSITY PRESS OF FLORIDA

Florida A&M University, Tallahassee
Florida Atlantic University, Boca Raton
Florida Gulf Coast University, Ft. Myers
Florida International University, Miami
Florida State University, Tallahassee
New College of Florida, Sarasota
University of Central Florida, Orlando
University of Florida, Gainesville
University of North Florida, Jacksonville
University of South Florida, Tampa
University of West Florida, Pensacola

Other books by Roy Gottfried from the University Press of Florida

*Joyce's Iritis and the Irritated Text: The Dis-lexic* Ulysses (1995)

*Joyce's Comic Portrait* (2000)

# Joyce's Misbelief

Roy Gottfried

Foreword by Sebastian D. G. Knowles

University Press of Florida
Gainesville/Tallahassee/Tampa/Boca Raton
Pensacola/Orlando/Miami/Jacksonville/Ft. Myers/Sarasota

Library of Congress Cataloging-in-Publication Data
Gottfried, Roy K.
Joyce's misbelief / Roy Gottfried ; foreword by Sebastian D. G. Knowles.
p. cm.—(Florida James Joyce series)
Includes bibliographical references and index.
ISBN 978-0-8130-3167-5 (acid-free paper)
1. Joyce, James, 1882–1941—Religion. 2. Christianity and literature—
Ireland—History—20th century. I. Title.
PR6019.O9Z555 2007
823.'912—dc22          2007027531

The University Press of Florida is the scholarly publishing agency
for the State University System of Florida, comprising Florida A&M
University, Florida Atlantic University, Florida Gulf Coast University,
Florida International University, Florida State University, New College of
Florida, University of Central Florida, University of Florida, University
of North Florida, University of South Florida, and University of West
Florida.

University Press of Florida
15 Northwest 15th Street
Gainesville, FL 32611-2079
http://www.upf.com

To Edward and Henry

# Contents

# Foreword

Joyce was not a good Catholic: this we knew. But now we have the data to back it up. What Roy Gottfried has done quite marvelously is demonstrate the precise nature of Joyce's rebellion against religious authority. *Non serviam* now has a fuller context: by reading Joyce against the Catholic doctrine of his time and through the versions of biblical texts that he chose both to use and to ignore, we now understand in particular terms the ways that Joyce distanced himself from the church. In a brilliant move, Gottfried measures Joyce's schismatic resistance against the *Catholic Encyclopedia*—prepared and serially published between 1905 and 1914 and spanning the period of Joyce's own catechism and education—to gauge his rhetoric against the doctrines he would have actually heard.

*Joyce's Misbelief* takes its lead from Gottfried's earlier prize-winning work on Joyce's language. In *Joyce's Iritis and the Irritated Text*, language is looked at from a slanted angle; here it is religion, and religious doctrine. Gottfried's approach is always to begin at the base level of text, and there are wonderful discourses here on the meanings of "gnomon," which is connected to *narrare* (to narrate), *epicleti* (given its Eucharistic sense of a summons or an initiation), and other cruxes in Joycean scholarship. The analysis of Joycean wordplay in this book is tremendous throughout.

Above all, Gottfried is an illuminator of text. His explanations of the distinctions between the Douay (Catholic) Bible and the King James (Anglican) Version are fascinating, and his dagger definitions of transubstantiation and consubstantiation are extraordinarily useful to anyone who, like me, still hasn't quite figured out the difference. Gottfried is good on all the heresies in the catalog; by situating Joyce within the heretical margins, he shows Joyce's abiding contempt for all forms of authority. Joyce is drawn to schism not just as a condition of questioning the church; the attractions of the Protestant Mass and the Authorized Version of the Bible are, as Gottfried shows, aesthetic. In the Protestant Mass the elements are metaphorical: the "is" of "This is my body" is not real, but figurative. (It is strangely comforting to know that, four centuries before the impeachment trial of President Clinton, there were public debates on the definition of the word "is.") Joyce's challenges to Catholic doctrine allow him, says Gottfried, to find "the form and figure of his art"; further, in Protestantism Joyce found an opportunity "to express more freely and openly transgressive and liberating ideas about sexuality, economics, and culture." Gottfried's close readings of "The Sisters," Stephen's sections of *Ulysses*, and the fable of "The Mookse and the Gripes" are revelatory: *Finnegans Wake* becomes the heretical act, the final assault on the authority of language, that Joyce was born to write. Heresy comes from the Greek word for choice (αἱρεσις). Joyce's choices, after reading *Joyce's Misbelief*, are never so clear.

Sebastian D. G. Knowles
Series editor

# 1

# Joyce's Misbelief

In "Telemachus," Haines asks Stephen a very direct question: "You're not a believer, are you? . . . I mean, a believer in the narrow sense of the word. Creation from nothing and miracles and a personal God" (U 1.611–13). Haines poses this question with the skepticism of the university man toward all notions of religion, rhetorically trying to include Stephen with his "are you?" Stephen's answer is less a personal than a logical one—"There's only one sense of the word, it seems to me" of believer; by so speaking he seeks to point out that to accept religious issues would be an unequivocal thought, that there is only one way to be a believer. Stephen does not think of himself as a believer, certainly not in the nearly creedal positions Haines suggests— "creation from nothing" and all that—with the "personal God" smacking more of a Protestant believer than a Catholic one. Joyce was also not a believer.

If one is not a believer, however, the options open are many. One might be an unbeliever, someone for whom religious issues and questions would have absolutely no weight or interest. Stephen is certainly not that; no one who could repeatedly entertain questions of the Trinity, or of church history, or of transubstantiation, could have any claim on agnostic unbelief. No one could be an unbeliever who would, as Joyce, refuse to take the Eucharist in a mime show of empty gesture. In *Portrait*, the following exchange brings out just this sense: "Do you believe in the eucharist? Cranly asked.—I do not, Stephen said.—Do you disbelieve, then?—I neither believe nor disbelieve in it, Stephen answered" (239). The reason Stephen will not communicate, argues Cranly, is that Stephen feels "that the host too may be the body and blood of the son of God and not a wafer of bread? And because you fear that it may be? Yes, said Stephen quietly. I feel that and I also fear it" (P 243). (This exchange seems to replicate an actual conversation with Stanislaus, as recorded in *My Brother's Keeper* [103]). As Stephen's disavowal indicates, his is not the position of an unbeliever.

If not an unbeliever, then a disbeliever: someone who would reject Christianity as Haines has laid it out (in the brief but rather catechetical terms of creation and salvation) and seek to deny those claims in favor of transcendent other ones. Theosophism lay readily to hand in Dublin, as did tantric Hinduism or esoteric Buddhism. These received nothing but Stephen's derision and Joyce's mockery. Stephen is not a disbeliever.

Were it posed to Joyce as it is to Stephen, the answer to Haines' question is what Joyce himself said he was, writing to Lady Gregory when he formed his necessary plan of exile from nation and home and religion: "Although I seem to have been driven out of my country here as a misbeliever I have found no man yet with a faith like mine" (*Letters* 1:53, n.d. [11/1902?]). While he seems to argue that his exile is imposed from without, rather than his own choice, the sentence clearly wants to be an exercise in martyrology; he is "driven out" because of his faith, first off presumably in himself, and secondly, against the church. There is no one with a faith like Joyce's, as we shall explore in this study, and that is because he is not a believer in Catholic pieties, not an unbeliever in the rich complexity of religious thought and symbol, nor a disbeliever in Catholicism in order to hold to another and alternate religious system, but a misbeliever, someone who does not think as others do about Catholicism, but who clearly thinks about it nonetheless. He will not believe, but he might believe in an unorthodox way; he cannot unbelieve, as the history of the church and its ritual are so clearly a meaningful exercise in thought and art, but he will not consent to them. He will not disbelieve, because other non-Western religions available to the literati were illogical and vain. He can only misbelieve, which is to consider the issues of his church and its tenets about the nature of God and the means of religious worship, and to consider them again and again all throughout his life and his works, but to consider them from a perspective, an angle, that is willfully driven just to the outside.

"Misbelief," the very term Joyce uses, suggests within itself a deep paradox and a tension—that of a faith, a doxology, but one held wrongly or askant. Misbelief requires, of course, the structure of belief.[1] One cannot take a misstep from the path without knowing what is the way. Orthodoxy is required in order to have heterodoxy; a unitary meaning must exist from which can be derived a more multiple, more complex heterodoxy. The rightness of belief marked in the two parts of the word "orthodoxy" leads by direct contrast to the two parts of the contrariness in "misbelief."

Orthodoxy is a standard, rigorously upheld; if not arbitrary, by virtue of being derived from a long-running dialectic of challenge and questioning, it is, however, intrinsically circular in the logic of its definition. The *Catholic Encyclopedia*, nearly contemporary with Joyce's education (and thus a source of dogma), asserts that "Orthodoxy . . . signifies right belief or purity of faith," and right belief is "in accordance with the teaching and direction of an absolute extrinsic authority" and "not merely subjective, as resting on personal knowledge and convictions."[2] Orthodoxy requires assent, self-denial, and submission (traits inimical to Joyce's character). Moreover, as the authority of the *Encyclopedia* continues, "he, therefore, is orthodox, whose faith coincides with the teachings of the Catholic Church" ("Orthodoxy," 11:330). Joyce wished rather to divaricate than coincide.

Orthodoxy is defined by "the example set by the Apostles and Early Fathers" (*CE*, "Orthodoxy")—something analogous to original intent in Constitutional arguments. Differences arise in interpretation of this intent, according to a popular catechism of the nineteenth century, when teachers "fall away" from authority presumably by exercising subjective interpretation and personal conviction; their falling away is defined, circularly, by their not adhering to the divine doctrine which is "always preserved . . . by the Infallible teaching body of the Church."[3] This body is self-regulating, made manifest in the "purity of faith and teaching," according to the *Encyclopedia* (turning to catch its own tail), "in its whole history, but especially in such champions of the faith . . . , in councils, condemnations of heresy, and its definitions of revealed truth" (11:330). Orthodoxy resides in the authority outside an individual; it is collective and incapable of error. To embrace the variety in other possibilities is to take a stance that resists subordination and asserts individuality.

Dogma evolves over time, as Joyce well knew and in knowing must have felt that each such development seriously called into question the very nature of revealed truth and authority's ability to pronounce on it. When in the story "Grace" (begun in 1905) Joyce has the characters recount the declaration in 1870 of papal infallibility, he does so not only to show their faulty memories and erroneous assumptions, but also because he saw that decision as representing the essential arbitrariness of authoritative pronouncements on dogma. If the Pope cannot proclaim a word of false doctrine ex cathedra, then the circularity inherent in orthodoxy—what is true is what is articulated by authority—is made most evident. Cunningham's account and the other characters' interpolations and interjections to it have many errors: misnaming, misattributions of ideas, inaccurate information. Joyce surrounds this "history" with error so as to demonstrate the weakness (the fallibility) of any chronicle of ideas and events and thus slyly to undermine the very means by which orthodoxy stakes its claim.

The decision of the Vatican Council is represented by Cunningham through an imagined pronouncement, "Credo," falsely attributed to an Irish archbishop who did not speak the phrase and was not present at the deliberation—the absent figure and empty phrase a way of suggesting Ireland's complicity with the decision. This declaration is instantly followed by Mr. Fogarty's helpful and wholly unnecessary translation, "I believe," and then repeated by Cunningham's "Credo." In this repetition alternating Latin and vernacular Joyce foregrounds the very issue so crucial to him, what he would not believe: not in authority, nor in its ability to pronounce on truth in any language, nor in the necessary submission. The idea of the Pope being infallible in matters of doctrine when he speaks officially was a long-held, tacit assumption, so that the Council's ratification of the idea in 1870 was itself a repetition that may have spoken to that body's need for assertion in a more contemporary world.[4] The idea of authority declaring its authority Joyce could not credit but only miscredit; papal infallibility for him displayed exactly all the self-evident constraints that he sought to challenge by adopting and replaying postures of apostasy.

Moreover, if self-regulating, orthodoxy is likewise self-defining. Even as Joyce uses the authority of the church so that he can by opposition find his identity in apostatic counterstance, the church, in its circular logic, has needed its heresies to define and to exercise its power. This necessity has been noted by Virginia Burrus: "Risking oversimplification, we may say that it is initially the discourse of orthodoxy engendered by an antignostic heresiology that seems to *supply* the church with its distinctive institutional structures and technologies of power" (356, italics in original). Burrus remarks further that this "discourse is also crucially the production of the orthodox 'subject,'" where "the object of knowledge is . . . both sharply delineated and duly transcendent in its purported unchanging purity, simultaneously revealed and reveiled within the containing structure of language itself—or, perhaps better yet, of textuality" (357). So by heresy is orthodoxy defined, its texts the expression of its subject position; so too, for Joyce, is his self-expression and his identity as an individual subject made through his embrace of heretical texts.

The education Joyce received in his religious training and in his culture (as summarized by the *Catholic Encyclopedia* and expressed in various catechisms) was one that stressed a single meaning, absolute and clear. It would provide him examples of the one true faith, whose terms he well knew but to which he could not assent. A misbeliever is one who engages the issues and tenets, the figures and forms of dogma, from a distance, a place that is off, separated. Misbelief shares with belief the same terms, the same facts of history, the same forms of worship, but wants to handle them differently, wrongly, of course, by slightly misapplying or misdirecting them. Joyce always returns to issues of the church (as no unbeliever or disbeliever would), to those large questions which challenge the orthodoxy of the "believer," because Joyce felt the unitary view of religion was so conscriptive and constricting. To be a misbeliever is to set oneself away from faith, alien from it, but always aware of its place, its shape and topology. Apostasy is literally a standing away, a conscious act of separation. Misbelief, looking always at unitary belief from afar and defining itself by that distance, is a sort of chosen exile. In that space of distance, of exile, is an openness crucial to Joyce's misbelief: he wants to challenge the "narrow" view of religion, the only definition of the believer, with an openness to possibilities of redirection.

That challenge is based, certainly, in Joyce's view that religion represents (and indeed is) a source of authority whose power derives particularly from such unitary and monolithic meaning. Against a monolith one must struggle mentally. The church with its dogma is an order that invites disorder; it is a history and chronicle and text that demands to be read, understood, and then challenged rather than served. Religion is for Joyce an intellectual problem, a challenge to all orders of epistemology, history, and culture.

If heresy provides choice and challenge and hence freedom for Joyce, it does so in a particular way by offering him a post-hoc position that has been fully rehearsed, chosen, and practiced. To adopt that already existing stance is to exercise an individual freedom by a sort of imitation and reenactment. In the patterns of doctrinal tradition, religious thinkers develop and maintain ideas that they themselves consider true and correct. That is to say, in the history of dogma, individuals held ideas they first took up not in order to be rebellious or confrontational, but because they considered them logically consistent and consequent. Most heretical movements did not start out as rebellions but as thoughtful developments, exercises in intellectual worship. The initial process is one of genuine searching for truth, an exercise in the freedom of intellectual thought granted to all. Choices are not initially known to be heretical but only become so. As has been noted in the *Encyclopedia*, unorthodox ideas come to be defined as "subjective" rather than "in accordance with . . . an absolute extrinsic authority" ("Orthodoxy" 11:330). It is only through the passage of time and interchange with other religious thinkers that ideas are judged to be unacceptable and condemned as anathema. In fact, Jaroslav Pelikan notes in *The Christian Tradition: A History of the Development of Dogma* that to understand "the present history of dogma," "one must read back from what was confessed" to what was initially believed.[5] Thus the declaration of heresy must always be post hoc. What is condemned is not the thinking but the thought after the fact; not the process but the result.

Once an idea is declared anathema, condemned by authority, to persist in it is, of course, to be an apostate; therein lies the choice designated by the meaning of heresy. Thus while the initial thinking may not intend to be schismatic, the *practice* of heresy, made after the fact, is intentional: it is a choice to embrace what has been declared wrong. Dogma recognizes this as "active" schism, "detaching oneself deliberately from the body of the Church" (*CE*, "Schism" 13:529). It is a stance whereby one wills to become an apostate, to stand off and away; it is to be "driven out," as Joyce wrote of himself to Lady Gregory.

For Joyce, the willing embrace of apostasy, his own sort of exile, is done precisely by acknowledging the belatedness of the actual historical determination of heresy, its post-factum quality; he seeks to stand in the space of schism already established by heresy. Unlike the theologian who only in time becomes a heretic, Joyce adopts what has already been declared as rebellion by authority and the body of the church. He comes long after the facts of previously made decisions in the "whole history" of the church "in councils [and] condemnations of heresy" (*CE*, "Orthodoxy"), choosing willingly to rebel. Not for him is it a choice made that only after the fact becomes a challenge; rather it is a challenge foremost and outright. It is precisely because he knows his choice is schismatic, because he makes his choice after the fact, that he is so attracted to making it. He freely, with his own cunning, replays the postures and rehearses the positions of historical heretics.

It does not require a history of heresy to chart Joyce's willful adoption of schism. His interest in particular heresies follows very much the main historical chronology of challenges to the one true faith (as we shall explore): Gnosticism, which was present even before there was a church;[6] Trinitarian controversies that dominated the early unified Christian world; the split between Constantinople and Rome, the first Great Schism; and the Protestant Reformation, the second. It is enough to note that he sought out those moments in order to engage in the openness already made available by the past. Because the church had already declared these ideas illicit, Joyce could replicate them in rebelliousness, imitating their challenges again as in the past.

It is informative to consider how tightly and firmly Joyce's interest in heresy, exactly because it was a post-hoc and deliberate choice, adheres to his practice of art. The actual historical heresies Joyce engages, because they belong to the passage of time and the slow and linear progress of acts and consequences, are a narrative, a sequence of events with their causes and effects. His embrace of heresy reads like a history, movement by movement: the Great Schism and the Reformation are his chosen stages. And his selected heresies are stages in another way. The replaying and reprising of the stances and postures are proscribed acts, dramatic in their intellectual gestures because conforming to a role; his rebelliousness is presented as something like a staged event, itself always already a *deroulement* after the fact of a script. Willing to plead *non serviam* is electing to perform the role of Lucifer.

To again think and create along the lines of something done before is not only to role-play but to imitate, and imitation is at the very core of Joyce's art. If in fact he argues in the Pola notebook that art imitates nature—and it would imitate life in the scrupulous meanness of his stories or the minute exactness of his novels—then it would imitate the tradition of apostasy against the church by resisting its power. Words and scenes and gestures recall moments of heresy, even as Joyce's heretical references call up again heresies long ago pronounced.

Joyce's retelling is an intellective version, consciously miscast, of what he had been told. The education Joyce received at the hands of the Jesuits may not have instilled in him abiding faith in its unity, but it did give him a rigorous sense of logic that made it impossible for him to completely turn against the careful defense of the Church Universal provided by the fathers and made it equally impossible for him to entertain any other transcendent claims (such as the fashionable spiritualism) because they had no intellectual weight. His interest in misbelief would be one as rigorous in its intellectual application as was the defense of orthodoxy within the history of the church. Stanislaus indicates the extent of Joyce's valuation: "The interest that my brother always retained in the philosophy of the Catholic Church sprang from the fact that he considered Catholic philosophy to be the most coherent attempt to establish . . . intellectual and material stability."[7] Faddishness and skepticism would not appeal to Joyce as the means to challenge Rome; only those deeply thought-out and consistent intellectual questions posed in history around the equally philosophical and scholastic heresies and historical schisms would serve. To return, early and late in his life, to questions such as those regarding transubstantiation or the procession of the Holy Ghost within the Trinity was not to embrace a Herbertian skepticism, nor to dismiss outright two thousand years of rigorous thought, but instead to look at them closely, if askance.

To think that way, with the power of the intellectual imagination, with the rigor of logic, and with the sanction of historical events, was to free himself from the authority of the church that was imposed upon him by his education and his culture. Misbelief wants to open up possibilities inherent in worship to freedoms of choice and application. By misbelieving, Joyce would preserve his own integrity: to be a misbeliever meant that he could engage the power of his mind by engaging as well the choice of his own intellect. That way led to a freedom he sought as a person and an artist. In challenging religion, he asserts himself against a powerful force that demanded he relinquish his own integrity. Not to serve did not mean to reject nor did it mean to substitute, but it did mean to follow through with what he calls a "faith like mine."

He would also resist those pieties and lesser orthodoxies that derived from claims of the church's authority. To misbelieve in the faith was, logically and necessarily, to misbelieve in those ideas that follow from it. Religion led to an ideology, and that ideology was firmly integrated with all that mattered to Joyce as an artist: choices of the individual self; the received ideas of culture; questions of the unknown and unforeseen in real life whose patterns the artist sets out to describe. Nationalism, which also influenced everything in his culture, was another monolithic force deriving its power in fact from its increasing alignment with the Roman Catholic faith. To such a power Joyce could not any more assent than to the church. Whatever demanded his loyalty he resisted by evasion, by challenge, by taking only part of its truth.

It should be noted that Joyce exercised misbelief in intellective and creative acts, not in social ones. Joyce did not misbelieve in his behavior: he was notable for his avoidance of blasphemy and foul language (even if his landlady in Zurich called him, presumably because of his "black goat's beard," Herr Satan).[8] He did not perform in darkened rooms and light candles in a sort of mischievous ritual as did Huysmans or Aleister Crowley. When invited to drink by the aggressive and predictably shocking Robert McAlmon with a call "Here's to sin," "Joyce looked up suddenly and declared, 'I won't drink to that.'"[9] (Joyce also described his drinking companions, not incongruously for him, as "beati innocenti.") His bearing and his manners were scrupulously correct, middle class, and not bohemian. It was his thinking that was forward and challenging. To misbelieve in thought was to exercise his own independence in the way that was most important to him, as something resembling cunning.

To do this, to be a misbeliever rather than a believer or an unbeliever was, for Joyce, to be always mindful of orthodoxy while attempting to break its hold of unitary meaning, its narrow sense, and to open up personal possibilities that led to artistic ones of rebellious challenge and freedom. When he conceded that "the whole of what" Wyndham Lewis had said in critique of Portrait was "true," Joyce also asked whether it was "more than ten per cent of the truth."[10] In this question, Joyce advanced the powerful argument that truth is not unitary and complete—his true reaction to what he had been taught by the catechism—but rather always partial and fragmented. Joyce's is not merely a question about literary judgment but a philosophical statement. There is something more to be seen, looked at askance, in order to disrupt power and challenge authority.

Thus it is that the historical model for Joyce is schism. Defined as an intentional and persistent resistance to orthodoxy, schism repeatedly will not submit or serve. The orthodox view, the one that insists on unitary meaning, is challenged, and the resultant schism is an assertion of difference and multiplicity. To be schismatic, however, still requires orthodoxy for its definition: no unbeliever can be a schismatic because orthodoxy can have no hold; no disbeliever can be a schismatic because orthodoxy must be rejected. Only the misbeliever can be the schismatic, because he takes orthodoxy seriously in order to dispute it and try to tear its unitary meaning. A schismatic is heretical in that he makes a choice to turn orthodoxy aside, to misdirect and replay it; a schismatic is a misbeliever according to orthodoxy and a free thinker according to his own lights.

It is the contention of this study that Joyce was concerned with religious ideas, never able to break away from their consideration, never able to break their powerful hold on his mind. He turns to them again and again early and late in his works, never able to either disprove or ignore them. Neither a disbeliever nor an unbeliever, but never able to be a believer, he misbelieves continually. His misbelief affords him possibilities of challenge, of openness, that all invigorate his artistic endeavors.

Joyce's misbelief takes the logical and necessary form of an interest in actual schisms in the history of the church that, as he himself does, took on the unitary thinking of its universal authority to challenge its premises, to redefine its claims. To do so, as did the Eastern Church or the Reformation ones, was never to be far from the claims of the Church Universal; indeed to be possible at all, schism must be very close to the ideas of the faith, but treat them differently, see in their changing challenge a possibility of freedom, of otherness, of newness. Joyce is attracted to schisms in the church because, as he rehearses them, they open up for him possibilities of his art.

The distance of misbelief from belief as a form of exile, the intellectual and logical response to orthodoxy as an act of true cunning, from this combined artistic aim and Trinitarian parallel the one missing element is silence. The next chapter begins with the way Joyce indirectly articulates his misbelief in the spaces of silence opened up by schism.

# "A Ripping Good Joke"

## The Attractions of Schism

Much in Joyce proceeds by indirection; what is crucial to the text and to him is often nudged to the side of the main attraction. Meaning is divertive in the sense that the ostensible focus of Joyce's narrative is often a substitute—a distraction, an amusement—for what is really at issue. Mockery and play are strategies of indirection, seeking to move away from something serious, to parody something essential. It is in the oblique spaces created by indirection and circumlocution that opportunities for freedom occur. Misbelief thrives in silence and misdirection.

Joyce's interest in religion is similarly expressed through indirection and deflection; it all begins with a joke. The Stephen Dedalus of *Portrait* is a character who, while constantly being schooled, alternates between religious impulses of obedience and rebellion; his interests and concerns are frequently about matters of faith. Because of his superior status as head boy, he is expected and called upon to act the part of a schoolmaster during Belvedere's Whitsuntide performance. Yet his part is just that—an act, a role-playing.[1] His concern for issues of obedience and faith are likewise called up when his schoolmate Heron suggests that his performance add a touch of parody: "What a lark it would be if you took off the rector in the part of the schoolmaster. It would be a ripping good joke" (75). The "lark" is the lightheartedness of a schoolboy prank (whatever its comic lowering of Stephen's self-conception in the later figure of the "hawk-like man"), and the imitation and parody of the august religious leader, his being "taken off," would be "ripping"—slang for something excellent, splendid. The inference is that all authority, teachers and priests both, should be ridiculed. Stephen is asked by Heron particularly to parody the rector's sonority: "*He that will not hear the churcha let him be to theea as the heathena and the publicana*" (76).[2] To jibe at authority, especially its pronouncements about serious matters, by mocking its voice, its pronunciation, is a fine piece of work.

A loose transcription of Jesus' words to his disciples about how they should regard rebellious congregation members, those who "will not hear," the statement Heron proposes for mocking the rector deserves attention. The passage from Matthew 18: 17 in the Douay Bible reads: "If he will not hear the church, let him be to thee as the heathen and publican." Heron is not quite accurate, although he gets close. The Authorized Version also approaches near enough: "But if he neglect to hear the church, let him be unto thee as an heathen and a publican." (There seems to be a little trouble about those articles, "the" and "a" publican. The fact that Joyce's text corresponds to neither version will be discussed later.) This sentence presents obliquely and silently something that is not foregrounded in the main narrative. Here, Heron persists in teasing Stephen, this time about Emma and how his erotic interest in her precludes him, according to Heron, from being a "saint" (77) and makes him rather a "sly dog" (76). Through Heron, Joyce continues to challenge and mock religious values, suggesting his own cynicism. When Heron forces Stephen to "admit" his hypocrisy, he "submissively"—if comically—recites the Confiteor.

The confession is the apparent focus both of this narrative sequence and the subsequent memory it evokes of a similar incident in which Stephen refuses to admit that Byron is a heretic; yet the passage Heron calls to be parodied is as much the issue as the succeeding scenes of mock confession and submission. The statement from the Gospel is one of the seminal directives on how the faithful should respond to a heretic. The *Catholic Encyclopedia* cites the same passage from Matthew to define heretical behavior ("Schism," 13:532). Heresy is a manner of thinking or following a school of thought, and the word derives from the word for choice, one of perversion *and* diversion. Even while Stephen is only "acting," he both defines heresy and pronounces on it. This choice and its tangential presentation in the text pertain to the essential identity of religion in Joyce, represented through imitation, parody, and indirection. On one side, religion is *relegere*: a rereading or an interpretative choice that repeats (hence, the imitation of the rector through play-acting or Stephen's repeated memories of conflicts with Heron.) Yet religion is also *religare*: a binding or restricting, something like a net that must be avoided or cut. In Stephen's Whitsuntide parody, Joyce employs narrative reproduction and repetition (relegere), while the oblique, divertive meaning of the Matthew passage breaks bonds, narrative and religious (religare).

It is heresy to which this episode and the two memories it evokes return, each scene a rereading of the previous one, each involving Stephen's retaking of a similar stance. And in each case, heresy is intimately connected to the power of literature. Thus the events at the school play evoke Stephen's memory of "another scene called up as if by magic" of reenactment—that is, by another performance involving illusion and imitation. The first episode recalls an earlier event in Stephen's life where, in the classroom, he is accused of heresy by the English master, Mr. Tate. The issue is one of both doctrine and diction, wrapped up together in literature. Stephen, "still smarting under . . . [a] squalid life," passes his time outside of school "in the company of subversive writers" whose "speech . . . passed into his crude writing" (78). His poverty and his errant, rebellious reading make him conscious of failure so that "he felt against his neck the raw edge of his turned and jagged collar," the very sort of binding and constriction represented by his religious education, as if the collar were a clerical one. The error of which Tate accuses him is, in fact, merely a lapse of the pen, Stephen's having written of the soul "without a possibility of ever approaching nearer" to God, when he meant "without a possibility of ever reaching"(79). He does not make a volitional statement of heresy, but a slip of the pen similar to Heron's inaccurate transmission of the Gospel passage. His "submission" of a correction to the instructor is the public equivalent of his "admission" to Heron. He acquiesces to authority; the "subversive writers" he has read have not as yet been enough to overthrow the powers of teacher and rector.

The conflation of things literary with things heretical continues in the narrative's elaboration of Stephen's recollections. A few nights after his public classroom chiding, he encounters the same Heron, who, with two dull acquaintances, asks Stephen to name the best poet. When Stephen chooses Byron, Heron challenges Stephen's religious belief, calling him a heretic and demanding, in a sort of literary auto-da-fé, that he confess his error. It is Heron who here associates religious purity with artistic taste, and Stephen seems glad of the opportunity to be a martyr. This earlier and first recital of the Confiteor is a "malignant" episode, where the confession before the school play is a comic one. The confession scene repeats—once as tragedy, once as farce.

With the cruelty that always accompanies coercion, Heron repeatedly demands that Stephen "admit" his strongly held conviction about Byron. As with the "submission" to Tate, admission of error is the remedy for heretical positions; it is to give in, to accept the strictures that bind one to faith.

Along with the conflation of heresy and literature—embodied in Stephen's essay for schoolmaster Tate and in Byron's poetry—imitations of belief, what we might call variations on the confessional gesture, figure prominently in *Portrait*'s heresy episodes: the joking (and thus ungenuine) contrition before the school play; the publicly expressed though coerced admission of error in the classroom; even Stephen's anticonfession, his refusal to sacrifice Byron to religious provincialism in a moment of martyrdom. Literature and heresy seem mutual in these scenes, and one's choice has artistic repercussions.

There is, however, more behind these scenes, something challenging and disruptive that has further consequences. Returning for a moment to consider what connects Stephen's memories, it is not the submission enacted in his recitation of the Confiteor, nor the accidental heresy inscribed in the essay for Tate, nor the refusal to admit any error in upholding heretical Byron. In other words, it is not associated ideas of heresy, complicity, and contrition that connect these scenes, but rather an accumulating pressure against ideological, artistic, and spiritual bondage. It is a wish (on Stephen's part, on Joyce's part) to release the strictures that maintain narrative repetition—those cycles of erroneous rereading, reinterpretation, and imitation—and to think freely, outside of convention and conventional wisdom. In short, it is the impulse to experience the kind of liberation suggested by the ripping quality of the "ripping good joke" that sets in motion the narrative sequence of recollected events and reiterations of positions already taken.

As the heresy scenes reenact each other through an ongoing narrative recorso of rereading and recreation, a textual tension builds between events that have already taken place and events repeated, between issues and positions already defined and those in process of redefinition. Joyce wants to present himself at places established as open, not in any way foreclosed. Freedom seems to reside with variations in repeated themes and sequences. Throughout the heresy passages, literature remains an open site through possibilities of parody and humor, the magic of memory and imitation, and infinite occasions for lapses in word choice. Narrative repetition is a form of *relegere*, a rereading of precedent to establish both orthodoxy and freedom. And within this recorso, heresy is as much a choice as Stephen's choice of Byron as best poet, and texts with errors, deliberate or accidental, are sites of "falling away." Literature plays an important constitutive part in expressions of heresy: it is on the basis of texts—through creeds, bulls, anathema—that heresy is defined and condemned.[3] The heresy scenes in *Portrait* suggest Joyce's abiding interest in those places where, through literature's narrative repetitions, variations, and wordplays, religion can be opened up and turned.

When Stephen refuses to admit that Byron is "no good" (82), he suffers punishment at Heron's hands. Pushed against a barbed wire fence, he is forced into reenactment—much as in the Whitsuntide play or in his memories—but in this case, reenactment of martyrdom: of St. Sebastian, where fence barbs replace arrows; of St. Stephen, where cabbage stumps replace rocks; of Jesus himself, where barbed wire echoes the crown of thorns. Stephen would clearly welcome such a figuration (if indeed he does not actively seek it), and Joyce considered himself a martyr, as he claims when he writes to Lady Gregory of having been "driven out" of Ireland. Pushed to his limit, Stephen "wrenched himself free. His tormentors set off towards Jones's Road, laughing and jeering at him, while he, torn and flushed and panting, stumbled after them" (82). This scene clearly functions in the text as an emblem: Stephen escapes restrictive coercion, violently liberating himself, withal the object of his tormentors' joke. He "stumbles" as if enacting a vignette of error and fall, and he is "torn" by this event, emotionally scarred. This episode is more malignant in its tones and contours than the episode on the evening before the school play. In the latter, the rector is the comic sacrifice. Here, Stephen is flayed for his faith in letters—his essay for Tate and Byron's poetry.

Yet it is through the literariness of Stephen's martyrdom—both his sacrifice for art and his sacrifice made into art—that Joyce transforms him by means of metaphoric substitution and synecdochic resemblance. Stephen is not in fact "torn," although his coat probably is. The rent in his garment has been prefigured by the "turned and jagged collar" of the same coat he wears in Tate's classroom. Stephen's poverty is indicated by the poor condition of his clothing, the jaggedness of a frayed collar turned for thrift (with its additional resemblance to a cleric's collar). More than an emblem of penury, however, the jagged collar suggests the torn, frayed condition of Stephen's beliefs in literature, faith, and in himself. This condition of rupture is reinforced by the image of Heron making a "cleft" in the air with his cane as he approaches Stephen (79). Throughout this passage, words of rupture in various participial forms recur: "ripping," "split," "cleft," "torn." These words objectify Joyce's keen interest in the possibilities of a "breaking through" that creates freedom and possibility, and they all are synonyms for schism. If one does not submit to authority, to the voice of the rector in the church, but even parodies it, persisting in heresy, then one produces a schism. Schism is the unstated, primary concern of the heresy scenes, where religious choice resides in literary gesture. And for Joyce, schism is the very means by which art is made.

While the absence of something can in logic rarely be used to prove its existence, it is worth noting in relation to Joyce's indirect presentation of the idea in the wings of *Portrait*'s heresy scenes that the word "schism" appears not at all in *Dubliners*, *Stephen Hero*, or *Ulysses*. (Heresies and heresiarchs appear five times in *Ulysses*, but never in *Dubliners* and *Stephen Hero*. In *Portrait*, heresy appears three times, all in the scenes we have examined heretofore). This absence (or better, this presence-by-implication-only) can be used to reinforce the claim that schism is in fact the focus of Joyce's religious concerns. It is perhaps a form of the "silence" he claims through Stephen is his artistic method. Schism, as a rupture between one position and another, is an empty space. Just as Joyce holds his fascination with religious ideas at a distance, approaching them through narrative subversions, he similarly keeps his concern with the issue of schism at one remove.

The one place in *Portrait* where the word "schism" *does* appear is in Stephen's meeting with the dean of studies. In this scene crucial to Stephen's articulation of his aesthetic, schism is enmeshed with ideas about literature. Stephen's and the dean's conversation is filled with the language of religion and art. Assessing the dean's character, Stephen views him with condescension: "with the same eyes as the elder brother in the parable may have turned on the prodigal" (189), Stephen thinks him "a late comer, a tardy spirit" and asks himself why the dean was moved to join the church. Was it because "he had come to the Church through a fine thread of reasoning upon deep questions," such as Stephen follows, on "insufflation, or the imposition of hands, or the procession of the Holy Ghost?" Stephen wonders whether the dean's conversion was emotional, a response to a sudden summons: "Had the Lord touched him and bidden him?" Or, Stephen wonders, had the dean wished to find Catholic certainty over Protestant sectarianism: "Had he felt the need of an implicit faith amid the . . . jargon of its turbulent schisms, six principle men, peculiar people, seed and snake baptists, supralapsarian dogmatists?" Stephen also likens the dean to Levi, called away from "sitting at receipt of custom" to become the disciple Matthew.

While the word "schism" appears to be a feature of the dean's earlier life as a dissenter (what Stephen refers to metonymically as the "zincroofed chapel"), parts of Stephen's questions themselves refer to schismatic issues, such as prelapsarian dogmatists—which for Catholics would be Jansenists—or the procession of the Holy Ghost, the position of the Eastern Orthodox Church (this last a question to which Joyce returns, as we shall see, in the *Wake*). Stephen sees many comical schisms in Protestantism—itself a schismatic position for Catholics—and he seems to push even further beyond the proscriptions of orthodoxy, as many of the particular exotic factionalisms ("seed and snake baptists") are even more distanced, more apostatic, by being American sectarianisms. Schisms have an appeal in that they provide many other potential splits.

One feature of Stephen's contempt for the dean must be his feeling that the dean becomes a convert in order to avoid the "turbulence" of schisms. Stephen, as shown by the way he formulates his questions, is attracted to them, and to the possibilities their turbulence might bring in their train. One reason for Stephen's interest in the dean at all is that he was a convert of the Oxford Movement *and* someone who followed Newman in breaking away from the Anglican Church, which might be a recovery for the Old Faith, but could also be seen as two complementary acts of schism and repetition. All forms of rupture and openness are attractive to Stephen, as they are to Joyce.[4] To choose schism, the ripping of orthodoxy, rather than to avoid it, is for Stephen an act of will and freedom. To occupy open textual spaces is to embrace the freedom that the dean so readily gives away, and such surrender is what Stephen dismisses. The opportunities that such ripping entails are many, and all contribute to Stephen's art: freedom of choice, resistance to authority, expressing personal identity against dominant ideas and assumptions.

Joyce also defines the consequences of schism through the figure of the rector whose delivery of the verse from Matthew Stephen is urged to parody during the Whitsuntide play. Father Henry was Joyce's actual rector at Belvedere, yet he is unnamed in *Portrait* despite being the target of Stephen's parodic, ripping joke. He is nonetheless a figure of some moment. In fact, he was a convert; Stanislaus called him "a fanatical convert from Protestantism."[5] So the figure of authority in Stephen's school, and the butt of the intended imitation, is also a figure of some inversion as a convert to the faith. (And Henry is not the only butt of the imitation; the convert dean of studies at University College Dublin [UCD] in *Portrait* is unnamed, but he is called Father Butt in *Stephen Hero* and is the one with whom Stephen has the exchange about aesthetic theory. Art, humor, and the possibilities for them through schism seem of a piece to Joyce.)

So the charges against Stephen in the three remembered scenes of commanded confession in *Portrait* may involve heresy, but the essential focus is schism. Though in its "Schism" entry, the *Catholic Encyclopedia* notes—without citation, as if it were a commonplace—that according to St. Jerome "heresy and schism go hand in hand," there is an essential difference between the two terms crucial to Joyce (13:529) and to which we alluded briefly in chapter 1. Heresy is the holding of an idea, an intellectual choice that initially may be considered in good faith and with good intent that is subsequently determined to be wrong. Schism, by contrast, is the willful and conscious persistence in an idea that has already been determined to be wrong; it is a stance taken (a parti pris) that embraces the contrariness of the position. This is what the Catholic church calls "active schism," "detaching oneself deliberately from the body of the Church" (*CE*, "Schism" 13:529). Much like the iterative mode of Stephen's "confessions" in *Portrait*'s heresy scenes, an element of repetition, as of a stance retaken, characterizes schism. Schism resides in a place outside of authority, through the activity of cleaving, and in the distinguished space opened by rupture. The Catholic Church acknowledges this as schism "pure and simple," "the rupture of the bond of subordination without an accompanying persistent error" (*CE*, "Schism" 13:529). To be a heretic is to argue *with* dogma in a dialogue, often with the sense of exploration and investigation of the truth. To be schismatic is to argue *against* dogma, resisting authority, insisting upon difference, and thus to embrace willingly and after the fact the freedom of the outside and opened space, in the broken ligatures of *re-ligare*. That is why Joyce called himself a misbeliever, rather than a disbeliever on whom there were no bonds to cut. And it is this sense of schism, rather than heresy itself, which is Joyce's focus. Heresy is an error in thinking, which might be amenable to correction or persuasion, but schism is a position willingly and consistently held. To be heretical is to err, but to be schismatic is to separate, to hold oneself aloof, and to be free. Essentially, schism is a persistent and willful challenge to the unity of the church and its authority (inveterate characteristics for Joyce); it is a position and a place outside, apostatic, a form of exile (indirectly signaled by silence, as Joyce never names "schism" overtly in his texts).

All heresies are defined post hoc, condemned after their practice. In fact, many heretics initially proceed from good will, conscience, and conviction, without intending to rebel. After meeting censure, they may persist in what is a matter of conscience. It is precisely Joyce's willing adoption of stances associated with schisms long ago determined that forms the essential gesture of his misbelief. He does not take a position that he feels is orthodox only to have it defined by authority as heretical, but rather deliberately chooses to engage in historical replaying of schismatic positions. That is why the performative aspect of the Whitsuntide play with its rebellion against authority and its polyvalent quotations from scripture so readily defines and depicts his schismatic misbelief. He does not seek to create new rebellions against the church, but is content to use the older ones, as his purpose is to recreate a space already removed from authority for his art that is already always defined as apostasy.

The unity of the church is understood from scripture as being "of the same mind" (1 Cor. 1:10), and obedience to it is shown by granting preeminence to its leaders. Such powerful unity and authority Joyce inveterately would resist. One key passage for issues of unity and obedience is the foundation of the one church with Peter, where the singular authority descends to all in succession—"That thou art Peter; and upon this rock I will build my church" (Douay, Matt. 16:18), this verse, of course, from the same Gospel as the sonorous rector's parodied passage on heresy (Matt. 18:17), the Gospel also of the publican-Levi-become-disciple-Matthew (Mark 2:14) to whom Stephen compares the dean of studies. It was Joyce's way to use this passage to explain his method in the *Wake*: "The Holy Roman Catholic Apostolic Church was built on a pun. It ought to be good enough for me."[6] Yet it was not merely to insist on the ludic quality of his work that Joyce made this claim, a diversionary tactic itself. It was also to contest the unity of the church and its meaning, because the pun, as a diversion, is subversive of unitary meaning and insists upon breaking it into multiple possibilities. Thus to engage in schism is to reject a universalist view and likewise to refuse subordination to it. These two characteristics, rejection of a single view and resistance to the powerful hierarchical authority that maintains it, would seem to define Joyce's attitude toward most things, literary as well as liturgical. This is why religion and the schisms within it are so crucial to him: because they are homologues to everything he would try to do. And that is why they persist: because they are the dynamic of all that he strove to create.

To see how persistent the schismatic appeal is for Joyce and how crucial to his art, let us take up again his early artistic achievement of the epiphany. I have no wish here to rehearse the long and detailed formalist critical history of epiphany in Joyce other than to note that epiphany has elements pertinent to my theme of how religious ideas, treated askance, create artistic opportunities for Joyce. Epiphany is clearly about something transcendent in the world the artist observes: the real world of people, events, and places engages something spiritual which illuminates them from behind or beyond, and the artist has a superior role in its revelation.[7] Literature and the liturgical combine here (as we have seen them do elsewhere). The epiphany describes a particular dynamic: a narrative scene sparsely depicted so that it may be apprehended as more than it seems.

Stanislaus observes that the epiphanies are observations "of slips and little errors and gestures . . . by which people betrayed the very things they were most careful to conceal."[8] Thus art becomes like the confessional that provokes the recital of the Confiteor: errors—like those informing Stephen's classroom heresy—reveal something meant to be displaced or hidden, like the veiled presence of schism in Joyce's texts. Epiphanies rip the veil from actions to reveal or confess a meaning at odds with what is professed; error is epiphany's method, and disclosing another truth is its goal. The gap between the banal in the epiphanic account and the putative deeper and hence truer meaning it manifests is the same space opened by schism. This epiphanic dynamic perfectly justifies one's being a schismatic: the actual opinion reveals the emptiness of the professed orthodox view.

*Stephen Hero* presents the notion of epiphany directly, whereas by comparison, and reenacting the way Joyce often diverts attention away from main ideas in his work, epiphanies occur but are not overtly mentioned in *Portrait*. The context in which the epiphany and its analysis occur in *Stephen Hero* is telling. Stephen's unease about Emma and her pious attitude toward his erotic advances initiates a period of turmoil and worse, as he is said to be "anathematising" her. In his wanderings past Eccles Street (a prefiguration surely!) he overhears a trivial incident, a moment which he would turn into an epiphany by writing it down and preserving it. With Cranly he discusses the workings of epiphany in terms of an unpromising glimpse at the Ballast Office clock. He explains how the act of focus epiphanizes the object and how the apprehension of that object leads to understanding of beauty as Aquinas defines it. What in

*Portrait* is an aesthetic discussion of beauty and ideation is originally in *Hero* an act that proceeds from an experience with religious suggestions, especially ones that arise from everyday events in the material world.

From the erotics of Emma to street incident to aesthetic theory moves a trajectory frequently encountered in Joyce's works. This sequence is much like that in *Portrait* where Heron's teasing Stephen about Emma leads first to his mock confession and then to memories of related events—the heresy scenes with Tate and Byron—all of which yield a glance at the schism lurking just to the side of the narrative main road. Emotions, especially erotic ones, lead finally to aesthetic appreciation and thought, all couched in religious terms.

The epiphany in *Hero* is itself instructive because its narrative moment concerns religion:

> The Young Lady—(drawling discreetly) . . . O, yes . . . I was . . . at the . . . cha . . . pel
>
> The Young Gentleman—(inaudibly) . . . I . . . (again inaudibly) . . . I . . .
>
> The Young Lady—(softly) . . . O . . . but you're . . . ve . . . ry . . . wick . . . ed. (211)

While the exchange is clearly flirtatious, the references are religious (the chapel), and being "wicked" indicates the transgressive. The everyday encounter of a generic young "gentleman" and "lady" reveals possibilities for error and breaking away. Joyce's original scene of epiphany contains traces of sin.

What needs to be recognized here is that the epiphany, whatever its artistic purpose and effect, has something to do with a religious sense, what Scholes and Kain call the epiphany's "spiritual properties."[9] Stanislaus also recognized this component; he describes the epiphanies as "revelations," a word as much eschatological as epistemological.[10] Most of them written early in Joyce's career, the sequenced epiphanies are meant to be interrelated Scholes and Kain argue; they resemble a sonnet or psalm collection, many of them directly treating religious matters. While surely the real world of Dublin they describe is itself always layered with religious concerns and conventions, the fact that Joyce chose the term "epiphany" indicates that he certainly intended to challenge conventional dogma. Epiphany 1 is the one first used in *Portrait*—a threat of eagles that "pull out [the] eyes" of unrepentant children—where authority bullies all forms of disobedience. Authority's voice is the dogma that must be resisted: that is the point of the "ripping good joke." Epiphany 6 is the vision of hell worked into Stephen's visceral response to the retreat sermon in chapter 3 of *Portrait*, as is, more distantly, the postcommunion scene of number 7. Several epiphanies are about the last things, particularly the illness, death, and funeral of James' brother George (19, 20, and 21). Religious ideas are mocked in number 10's presentation of a priest's poetry writing. Even as early as epiphany number 2, and based on as simple an act as reading (perhaps because it *is* an act of reading), Joyce makes recourse to religious terms: "It pleases me to read of [the] ways [of those in Alsace]; through them I seem to touch the life of a land beyond them to enter into communion. . . . Our lives are still sacred in their intimate sympathies."[11] To connect reading with a sacrament like communion is to reinforce the heretical choice of epiphany as a literary form in a willful act of displacement and misplacement.

The final point to note is that "epiphany" is a curious term for Joyce to have adopted: not in its sense of a manifestation or revelation, but in Joyce's usage—first for being religious at all and second because he connects it to motions of concealment, error, and transgression. While the Feast of the Epiphany is a particular event (and Joyce would have been familiar with it through the *Sodality Manual*),[12] the concept of epiphany as a revelatory manifestation, as Joyce must have known, "had its origin in the Eastern Church" (*CE*, "Epiphany" 5:504); that is a clear appeal to an origin far beyond the borders of his school's authority.

Joyce appropriates elements from religious ideas, which he adapts quite freely so as to break willingly from authority and tradition to establish something of his own. This is a schismatic move, and it is the sort of thing we will see him do repeatedly. To call these vignettes "epiphanies" (and remember, one of his earliest projected works was to be called "Vignettes") is to arrogate to himself something of the sacramental for his own, not the church's, purposes. It is less important here to consider his purposes for doing so (those have certainly been covered) than to note that he has taken and reapplied religious terms in order to gain certain artistic options and freedoms. This is the attraction of schism.

Similarly, using "epicleti" (by which he meant "epiclesis" as we shall explore in the next chapter) to describe the form of his first published stories, Joyce made a similar move, even more pointed because the epiclesis is in fact one of the causes of the actual, historical schism in the Eastern Church. To appropriate to himself these ideas is to be himself the leading center of meaning, to take to himself the issues of the Catholic Church and make them his own, what he will call in the *Wake* the "authordux" (425.20): the author leading away (Latin *duco*) into the possibilities of openness which is schism; the author becoming his own leader by the freedom of his breaking away. One might say that all of Joyce's work is an exercise of "schisthematic" (*FW* 424.36), a way of ripping up ideas to produce in art a thematics of possibilities.

Not only to be an author but also to make his own orthodoxy, this leading away by the "authordux" is Joyce's way with religion, and it is schismatic to the core. He appropriates religious ideas such as epiphany from the Catholic Church and uses them not to convey their own dogmatic meaning, and not merely to assert through metaphor his own identity as an artist (although that, too), but to break with authority and yet retain some sense of the spiritual for his own purposes.

Such breaking of dogmatic authority and its resulting thematic possibilities run through Joyce's career. Although the bulk of this project will engage some of these breaks more fully, let us follow up one small thread. What Stephen means by his epiphany is certainly a "manifestation" of a "sudden spiritual sort" (*SH* 211), but the Feast of the Epiphany in the orthodoxy of the church is concerned with the appearance of the Magi. Joyce intends, rather, with his appropriation of epiphany to stress the reflecting, narrating observer. In response to both orthodoxies, East and West, Joyce changes the focus of the moment. The Magi, according to the account in Matthew 2, follow a sign that directs them to a place and to a collective visit; they bring gifts but no commentary other than that suggested by their general attendance. By contrast, Joyce's epiphany—the manifestation of something spiritual rendered as an event revealed to one individual in a common setting—is a very particular enterprise of reflection and awareness. It has the focus of a conscious narration.

Joyce might have found a model for this sort of apprehension in a different religious scene from the Gospel of Luke: Simeon's experience at the presentation of the infant Jesus in the temple. (The stories of the Magi and Simeon are both post-Nativity accounts.) Moreover, that incident (like Joyce's epiphanies) is a model of all narrative: an account of someone's experience and a commentary on that experience—narrative of the sort that is the main activity of Joyce's art in all its various forms and lengths. At the temple, Simeon is able to see "with his own eyes" the Lord's anointed in the insignificant baby, an observation that reveals something beyond the surface reality as Joyce's epiphanies and all narratives are supposed to do. Simeon's subsequent commentary combines both his own reaction to the event and an indication of what will unfold in the future, an omniscient narrative prognostication: "Because my eyes have seen thy salvation . . . a light to the revelation of the Gentiles, and the glory of thy people Israel" (Douay, *Luke* 2:30–32). "Revelation" is the very term Stanislaus used to describe the epiphanies. This passage is called, from its beginning in the Vulgate, the famous Nunc Dimittis (Luke 2:29–32): "Now thou dost dismiss thy servant, O Lord, according to thy word in peace." Simeon has witnessed a sudden manifestation of spiritual promise in the form of a small infant brought for an established ritual, a commonplace Hebrew observance for every first-born man-child. This sudden appearance indicates a promise and a future, a sequence which forms the principal narrative pattern of the scriptures. (And it is the meaningful quality of narrative that is Joyce's concern in the epiphany and also what must have distinguished Simeon's scene for him.)

The feast commemorating Simeon's vision of Christ's "light" in an obscure infant is called Candlemas, and its date, meaningfully, is February 2nd, a date of major interest to Joyce. With what appears to be a characteristic touch of egotism, Joyce always valued his birth date and invested it with much meaning.[13] (Joyce's birthday is thus freighted with several conflated issues, a fact congenial to his mind, and those issues connect to Joyce's art, a fact flattering to his ego.) In this context, let us raise another issue of long history in Joyce criticism—the superstition with which Joyce regarded his birthday—and return it to both a sort of freewheeling worship and to his appropriated notion of epiphany.

Joyce always lit a candle to St. Lucy on February 2nd, although the virgin martyr's feast day is December 13th.[14] St. Lucy is associated with candles and lamps because of the linguistic connection between Lucia/lux. Through such connections, words yield revealed meanings beyond their commonplace ones in a transaction similar to that at play in Joyce's literary epiphanies. Only the Gospel of Luke records the presentation of Christ in the temple. To the linguistic partnering of Lucia/lux, we can add Lucan (from the gospeller Luke), forming a string which seems to confirm Joyce's predilection for signaling his presence in the flesh along with the various spiritual agencies deployed by him. He takes several religious feasts and places himself in them: that is the way, by breaking with orthodoxy, to open up possibilities for his art.

Joyce's proceeding this way, by associations of words that reveal a meaningful and united spiritual agency apparently medieval in its insistence on the connection of the temporal to the spiritual life, also indicates what he intends to show by the concept of epiphany itself: meaning suddenly revealed through the commonplace of words.[15] And this surely is another way in which he leads away from established dogmatic notions and church calendars into his own "authorduxy." But there is more leading away here as well: as Lucia is connected to lux and thence to Luke, so Simeon is echoic of Simon. And Simon evokes two other primal issues in Joyce's art of the spiritual and schismatic.

Simon is the name chosen for the fictional father; surely not enough has been made of this telling fact. When Simon tells the barmaids in "Sirens" that he was christened "Simple Simon" (*U* 11.207), you may be sure that the diversionary aspect of Joyce's art is at work. There must be something more here. Unlikely to be named for the apostle Simon Peter, a wholly orthodox move whatever its ironic effect, Stephen's fictional father might be named for Simon Magus.[16] It would compromise and, in characteristic Joycean fashion, complicate the symbolic father in *Portrait*—glossing the Dedalean craftsman into a fabled but failed magician who (in later texts, such as Pseudo-Marcellus' *Passio sanctorum Petri et Pauli*) tries to fly but unaided by the Holy Spirit falls and breaks his neck. The magician of Acts is someone who seeks to make himself greater than he is, a showman of sorts, much as Stephen describes his Simon as "a praiser of his own past" (*P* 241).

That Stephen's name comes from Acts also suggests Simon's name has its origin there too. As "Dedalus" suggests the artist as forger, the sham and shaman Simon also is present. Simon Magus tried to buy the gifts of the apostles and fly. His fall links him to the failed son Icarus. Simon Magus is the source of the name for the sin of simony, so that the father is a spiritual source of the transgressive and the rupturing in the very biological creation of the artist. And simony, by this sort of similitude, is itself a kind of purchase of artistry and magic, an appropriation of the gift of the spirit. Simony, while not an act of schism, is a sin of inauthenticity, an attempt to achieve "authorduxy." Not surprisingly, then, simony is the original lapse (or source sin) which in Joyce's aesthetic makes art possible, a lapse foregrounded in the very first story of *Dubliners*, "The Sisters."

Joyce constantly rends and opens up texts and words, mining them for material from which to forge new associations. This is one way to challenge the unity of voice of authority and orthodoxy. As Simeon splits and links to Simon and Simon to simony, through a semantic chain of associations forged in the logic of schismatic thought, so too a similar move of rending and reconnecting may also be at work in the story in which the word "simony" appears. As Joyce's first appearance in print, "The Sisters" also marks the first appearance of his persistent tendency toward splitting, strategic indirection, and creative reassembly that characterize the narrative process described above for *Portrait*. (I will return to this story in chapter 3 to discuss why Joyce calls it and the other stories of *Dubliners* by the strange term "epicleti." Here I wish to examine only the notion of the schismatic that hovers throughout the text.)

First off, of course, the signal chalice that Father Flynn drops that "broke" is a sure sign of rupture. Then, from the trinity of words which mystify the boy, all seemingly hierophantic in their obscurity and with their possible meanings occluded from him, the odd word "gnomon" stands out. As with "paralysis" and "simony," this word too may possibly be misconstrued by the boy as a word from orthodox religious instruction. The boy has a tendency to such error and indirection in his apprehension of the world through language (indirection and error the very qualities that characterize Stephen's schismatic moments in *Portrait*). Many words he does not understand at all or understands only vaguely. For example, when he sees Father Flynn's corpse laid out in the vestments for the Mass, the boy remarks that his face was "massive" and his body "solemn and copious" (D 14). These terms relate to physical properties, much like the "work" of paralysis on the priest's body, but surely what eludes the boy is the spiritual meaning surrounding the words as articles of the faith. The "solemn" body is certainly the tonal solemnity in the mystery of the Mass the priest has sought to instill in him, and the adjective "massive" must certainly arise from that implicit connection. Likewise, by the same associative logic of the boy's confusion, "copious" must connect with one of the vestments in which the priest is laid out, the cope.

As a figure from geometry, the word "gnomon" denotes a parallelogram with a piece taken out of it—a rupture in shape. Yet "gnomon" may not come from this description by Euclid, but from something less material. The word may be found indirectly in the catechism in another form, and it might refer to something spiritual and threatening—gnosis or Gnosticism. Long before the established church, Gnosticism was an original schismatic movement.[17] It was challenged by the same "Fathers of the Church" the priest tells the boy wrote large books (Irenaeus, for one, who is mentioned in the *Wake*). The *Catholic Encyclopedia* maintains in its entry that Gnosticism was "oriental . . . to the core" (6:592), and the boy seems to allude to this origin when he dreams of the simoniac "far away, in some land where customs were strange" (D 14), like Persia. (Parseeism is generally often associated with Gnosticism.) The "strange" quality clearly suggests to the boy something forbidden and alien; it is something that, while remote, wavers on the edge—the dangerous brink of heresy, of open space, of artistic possibility—that defines the rending creativity of the schismatic.

The corpse of the priest presides over the story like a dead weight of authority and dogma. His instruction for the boy is the law (Restuccia clearly makes this connection in *Law of the Father*).[18] The wish for the father to be dead, to be gone, is a wish that not only pertains to Flynn but also, in the wonderful strange alchemy of the story, to the father in fiction of Simon, derived confusedly from "simony." The death of all fathers, such as those church fathers who write books as thick as the post office directory, would mean a break with orthodoxy; would mean freedom from the need to subordinate; would deny authority once and for all. It would be fully schismatic. The boy in the story "discovered in myself a sensation of freedom as if I had been freed from something by his death" (D 12). The freedom he finds "in himself" is the openness that Joyce sought from orthodoxy though appeal to schism; it is the operation of his own will.

Simony and Gnosticism, hidden among other words but revealed in flashes to readers, and epiphany, as defined by Joyce, representationally hover on the edge of splitting from Rome and thereby opening his works to allow for the possibilities of his narrative practice. Joyce was concerned with the two major historical breaks from the Church of Rome, the East–West Schism (or Great Schism) and the Protestant Reformation, and with the various consequences and changes these divisions spurred. These were historical challenges to the unity and power of Rome, events in time that for Joyce modeled the motions of his own artistic development. Whatever the beliefs that prompted them, these challenges involved intellectual stands, positions taken in the world of ideas, and Joyce was well aware that the intellectual imagination, as Stephen calls it in "Circe," is always called to take such stands in the courses of individual and world history. The East–West and Protestant schisms were crucial disruptions, even revolutions, and much of Joyce's work seeks out disruptions, be they in language, in culture, in gender, or in belief.[19]

By willfully reenacting the schisms of the remote past, Joyce fortifies his alliance with them. Invoking a long history of religious challenge, Joyce, in various forms and gestures, returns again and again to these actual historical schisms. As he replays them, he reinvigorates the past, rereading it as it were by his own *relegere*, his own misbelief. The earliest heresy that Joyce revisits casts its shadow, in the figure of the gnomon, over "The Sisters." Similarly, references to the Eastern Church's great split with Rome appear early and late in Joyce's works. The *Wake*, for example, plays with the concern for the filioque clause or the procession of the Holy Ghost—a difference between the Catholic (Western) and Eastern Orthodox traditions—as part, but not the cause, of their rift. The notion of epiclesis, pertaining to the invocation of the Holy Ghost to sanctify the elements at the Eucharist, is crucial to Eastern ritual and one of the major causes of the spit between Constantinople and Rome. Joyce evokes the rupture over the epiclesis most sharply in his own work when he uses the term to describe the stories of his Dubliners. It is not accidental that Joyce would have chosen this term to describe the narrative so as to make it rebellious and different. By making the stories strange, he breaks with the dogma of his religious instruction and the conventionality of fiction at one and the same time.

Epiclesis not only represents a position at odds with the Catholic Church of Joyce's day, a position which furthers his interest in the Eastern Church, it is also twinned with Joyce's interest in schismatic Protestantism, the second great split in the Roman Church based on the unorthodox reformist position that the elements of the Mass are emblematic rather than actual. This unortho-dox view of the Eucharist as a system of resemblances and metaphors enters Joyce's stories as a very close association of religion with art, and even with parody—the original impulse behind "taking off" the rector's authority in a "ripping good joke."

With schism in view, Protestant elements hover over parts of *Portrait* as we have already discussed. The dean of studies makes Stephen ponder the Oxford Movement, that return from schism, and his description of the dean's preconversion background invokes the often-fractious factions seemingly inherent in Protestant worship—its constant splitting into, among other sects, those "snake and seed baptists" that emblematize dissent (if not actually schism) within the established church as well as within more mainstream American splinter groups. As we noted earlier, when Heron inaccurately quotes the passage from Matthew which is to form Stephen's jest, his verse comes neither from the Catholic English Bible nor the Authorized Anglican one. Similarly, when Stephen likens the dean in his former state to Levi "sitting at receipt of custom," we cannot know with certainty whether he alludes to the Bible of the Catholic Church or that of the Crown. Allusion to scripture that leans away from the Bible approved for and frequently read by Catholics and leans toward the Authorized Version read closely and often by British subjects and members of the Anglican Church is another schismatic move for Joyce. We shall see how he flirts with such disruption by allusion to the King James Version, a tactic against Catholic orthodoxy marshaled in defiance of his nation's dogmatic resistance to British culture. It is important to remember that any choice of the English Bible on Joyce's part (choice being of course the hallmark of heresy) is a form of transgression, an alliance, albeit temporary, with a church that regards itself as part of the unbroken apostolic succession but which, seen from Rome, is schismatic. Such choice also signals Joyce's provocative alliance with Britain as the dominant imperial culture. As we progress, we shall trace the ways the *Wake* echoes the Anglican Book of Common Prayer, a move on Joyce's part which is striking in two ways: first as an allusion to another text arising from a clear historical split with Rome (an especially English split as opposed to a larger but generally Protestant one) and second as a challenge to Rome's use of Latin in those places where the Book of Common Prayer presents word-for-word translation of the Latin Mass into the vernacular.

Schism encapsulates all of Joyce's motives as an artist: release from intellectual and social conventions and thus freedom from their power. His return to and reenactment of historical schisms furnishes him with an established narrative set in historical time and imbued by a theme of rebellion. In art Joyce sought to relax literary conventions, linguistic forms, and social norms; through art he sought to sever ties to nation, to imperialism, to whatever constituted the constraints of power in the order of historical events.

Just as the name Gabriel in "The Dead" points to the paradox of the last days, so Joyce's view is always long, from early to end time. Eschatological history is always present in his texts, perhaps the most lasting legacy of his interest in religion. Schism is often implied obliquely in narrative incidents that themselves have historical moment, such as the reference in *Portrait* to a time early in Stephen's life when Dante had "ripped the green velvet back off the brush that was for Parnell one day with her scissors" (6). History for Joyce is always made up of moments of breaking, of death by sacrifice (the knife of politics Stephen notes in "Eumaeus"), or of tearing. In the history of the faith there are major heresies—those of Sabellius and Arius, for example—and great schisms—those of the Eastern Church and the Protestant Reformation. Not surprisingly, each plays out in Joyce's writing, early and late.

So schism is an essential idea in Joyce. It is "ripping" in the sense of freedom to split from authoritative orthodoxies, but also in the sense of splendid fun or play, like the proposed parody of the rector in *Portrait*. To break with practice, policy, and dogma for Joyce is to earn or seize for oneself much license and freedom. Schism from his national church and his family identity was precondition for Joyce to all he would practice as an artist. Not because he had to get out from beneath the church to *be* an artist, but because his act of schism was the means by which he would repeatedly *act* as an artist. That is why schismatic notions appear so often as concerns in his texts. A focus on religious schism gave Joyce intellectual freedom from dogma and papal authority, and those ruptures freed him from all analogous constraints.

# 3

# "Epicleti"

## The Artistic Possibilities of Schism

### 1

In the beginning of Joyce's creation there is a word, the substance of which is heretical, and that word is "epicleti." It is a word that initiates a body of works, the stories of the *Dubliners*, and it is a word that signals a disposition toward the possibilities of schism from the very outset. The word is something of a crux: a nonce word taken first as a religious term and more recently, in revision, suggested as a literary one; but in neither case has its meaning and consequences been considered. In a book about schism, the word "epicleti" requires some exegesis, because it marks a major rupture in religious history and provides Joyce with literary possibilities congenial to his interest in art and in misbelief.

The passage in which this strange word appears has become so familiar that it seems to have fallen beneath notice as if by a habitual critical paralysis. In a letter to his college classmate Constantine Curran in 1904, Joyce asserts his intent "to write a series of epicleti—ten—for a paper. I have written one. I call the series Dubliners to betray the soul of that hemiplegia or paralysis which many consider a city" (*Letters* 1:55). This clear statement of intent (perhaps too clear and confident) has always been glossed with regard to its thematic focus as a plan for a series of stories depicting physical inaction. And this intent has received, of course, excessive attention; the theme of paralysis has always made the easiest approach to the *Dubliners*. The additional purpose of exposing a city has its origins in Zola's naturalism and Ibsen's clinical diagnostic scrutiny.[1] Critics frequently note the planned aspect of the stories as a "series," marshaled out in parts to make a whole. (We will revisit this idea, as it speaks to Joyce's firm sense of a narrative sequence.) Another key theme in *Dubliners* is betrayal. A central issue for Joyce, this word which immediately evokes the politics of Parnell never loses its religious sense as one of the actions preceding Christ's Passion. Thus, Joyce's claim "to betray the soul" has in its literary focus a residual spiritual error such as "simony," a heretical choice. In short, the "epicleti" passage from his 1904 letter has been used to explain that Joyce has an aim in writing consonant with various formal and thematic purposes.

Critical habit notwithstanding, the term "epicleti"—of which this series is said by Joyce to be comprised—may signal an important approach to *Dubliners* and much else in Joyce.

As to what "epicleti" might mean, the literary and religious interpretations insist on their respective claims without considering what purpose Joyce had in using the term and what consequence he might have intended by it. If previously the word was taken from Stuart Gilbert, Ellmann, and Scholes in unquestioned (and unexamined) literary orthodoxy as something religious (and we will return to this claim later), since Gabler's 1993 edition of the *Dubliners*, the thematic aspect of the word has informed the current, unchallenged interpretation. In that edition, Gabler claimed that "epicleti" had been misread—understandably given Joyce's difficult, even hieroglyphic, handwriting. Now that the original lettering could be read definitively, Gabler, crediting Wolfhard Steppe, asserted that the word should be "epiclets," a diminutive of epic.[2] This reading, however, raises its own questions: "epiclets" seems to be a contradiction, a short version of what is formally a long narrative (and the epic derives from επος—word, utterance, poem—unrelated to epiclesis and never found as a diminutive). "Epiclets," too, is a solecism, compounding error upon error: if "epicleti" is bad Greek—and it surely is—"epiclets" is worse English. In 1904, Joyce had hardly any acquaintance with Greek, but he already possessed a firm sense of English.[3]

While it is a pat coincidence that the *Dubliners*, as brief epics, was supposed to include the story that was later transformed into the large epic novel *Ulysses*, the argument proceeds backwards from effects to causes and it does so by ignoring two issues. The first involves that other Greek word in Joyce's letter to Curran: "hemiplegia," a synonym for paralysis. Its presence reinforces the propriety of reading "epicleti" as a (nearly) Greek word. Greek is a nod to otherness (and to superiority, as Professor MacHugh claims in "Aeolus"); the aura of Greek words is essential to the opening of the first story of *Dubliners* with its enigmatic "gnomon." The otherness is precisely what appealed to the young Joyce in his wish for heretical options: otherness as a challenge to convention.

With stories entitled "Grace" and (originally) "All Hallows," and intended others "Christmas Eve" and "The Last Supper," an aura of religion surrounds the series, just as it does the word "epicleti." The flaw in earlier and established critical readings of the religious sense of "epicleti" is that they don't consider what was at stake in Joyce's very conscious use of the term. From the original publication of the 1904 letter by Gilbert in 1957 and bolstered by the authoritative word of Ellmann, the word has been understood *as* "epicleti" (not "epi-clets"), a nonce noun derived, apparently without any linguistic rules, from the Greek "epiclesis," itself derived from επικαλέω—to call upon, adjure, summon, quite literally as in invocation.[4] It is curious that the word was early and readily understood to refer to a spiritual matter, but the sense that it was renegade in Catholic orthodoxy was unremarked. Scholes notes, "this word may refer to an invocation to the Holy Ghost . . . still used in the Eastern Church but not in Roman Catholic Ritual. In this epiclesis the Holy Ghost is besought to trans-form the consecrated wafer of bread and the wine into the body and blood of Christ."[5] Such a gloss would seem likely, given Scholes' extensive work on the epiphanies in the notebooks and his claim to their "spirituality."

Any discussion of the actual status of the epiclesis in religious dogma, how-ever, is uninvestigated by Scholes; his defining the term as not used "in the Roman Catholic Ritual" merely begs the point. To accept the word as religious and not to see it as problematic is to miss a quality Joyce clearly intended by its use in the letter to Curran, a quality of the religiously subversive. While Scholes lightly touches on this difference by noting that the epiclesis is "still used in the Eastern Church, but not in Roman Catholic Ritual," he fails to de-velop the interpretative consequences; for Joyce they mattered. Epiclesis and the difference it marks in ritual are matters of schismatic effect. By referring to a term from liturgy—and doing so in the earliest literary explanations of his first stories— Joyce demonstrates that art is achieved by means of a challenge and a freedom made possible by schismatic religious issues and stances. The consequences of epiclesis figure in the two great schisms of the Roman Church: foremost epiclesis itself in the break by the Eastern Church; and secondly, in the changes in the nature of that Eucharist, the schism of the Reformation. Early on, to distinguish and define his art, Joyce aligns his writing with major historical ruptures in the fabric of the faith he had been taught at Clongowes and Belvedere. Epiclesis is not an empty word to use as the description of his first stories, nor is it formalism.

The Great Schism of the Eastern Church, like the schism caused by the Protestant Reformation, had many causes, among them notions of centralized authority, political power, and local identity that all appealed to Joyce in his condition as a subject of the Crown and as a servant of the church (issues we shall discuss in chapter 5). Joyce focuses on epiclesis as a means to articulate the splits motivated by history in the art he seeks to create. Because epiclesis refers to very substantial issues regarding the transformation of words into substances described in narrative, it concerns appearance and representation in art. Joyce writes a word to Curran that Curran is likely to find unfamiliar; Joyce uses it, however, not merely to take on that air of intellectualism he habitually assumed with his correspondents but rather to signal a complex series of issues he wishes to claim for an art schismatic at its very inception in 1904. Especially as epiclesis is an issue which challenges accepted Catholic doctrine, we have early on in Joyce's writing life a whiff of that ever-present brimstone of Joyce's interest in schismatic rending. The word "epicleti" in its meaning, its errant denotation, and its misuse is a challenge to orthodoxy in religion and art at the very onset of Joyce's writing career. "Epicleti" is bad Greek, but "epiclesis" raises philosophical and historical questions, profound with intellectual challenges to religious thought. Such provocations and possibilities are far more consequential than the formalist achievement of calling the stories little epics or the simple definition from Scholes that the term is liturgical. Joyce did not idly use the term but did so in order to call up—the very meaning of ἐπικαλέω—something that would be disruptive and alien and for that very reason would lead to the freedom of artistic possibility.

Not in any way a correct plural noun, the last syllable of "epicleti" sounds suspiciously like the Italian Joyce had studied at University College (perhaps he misconstructs "epicleti" because of that study). It is in Italy that Joyce makes clear the religious consequences of this word and its particular connection to the first story of *Dubliners*. When Joyce is in Rome, he writes to Stanislaus and makes an interesting self-satisfied pronouncement about the story "The Sisters" (the one of the series of ten he had already written, he told Curran): "While I was attending the Greek mass here last Sunday it seemed to me that my story The Sisters was rather remarkable" (*Letters* 2:86). "The Sisters" is the first of the "epicleti," and Joyce connects it to the Mass and the alienating schismatic identity of the Greek Church. In this association of Mass and story he thus clearly and unequivocally substantiates the Eucharistic associations of the term "epicleti" pertinently and logically, as the epiclesis is a feature of schismatic Eastern worship. This consistency seems to make a reading of "epicleti" as signifying "epiclesis" as much of a certainty as can be had in this fallible world.

We will gloss over the rather precise word "attending" Joyce uses to describe his going to Mass: it suggests that he was doing far more than watching a spectacle (although he was doing that, too) but that he was engaged in it—attending being an appropriate term for religious participation in the mystery. It suits Joyce's intent to move away from the Latin Mass.[6] He goes on to say, "The Greek mass is strange" (*Letters* 2:86). This is literally true, as Eastern Orthodox worship would be alien to one raised in the Roman Catholic tradition. Why Joyce sought out this unfamiliar exercise is worth considering. He did so repeatedly (see *Letters* 2:89, where he describes himself as "moping in and out of churches") as an act of apostasy to his taught doctrine; through a wish to transgress; and yet withal in a service of ritual in spiritual matters clearly schismatic. Ironically, the Eastern Church made claims to primacy in authenticity of worship, arguing that it was closer to the original church; so perhaps Joyce was trying to outflank the claim of the Catholic Church to primacy. He was certainly seeking to be contrary, to be alien to his upbringing. Joyce's purpose, however, was not merely apostasy in performance; it was to ground the origin of his art in considered rebellion and misbelief in religion. In short, "The Sisters" is his initial means to treat the issues of religion with a studied misbelief.

Thus the small and incorrect word "epicleti" works very large consequences in the areas of religion and art, the first in rupture with Roman orthodoxy pure and simple, the second in the conception of an art modeled on the notion of epiclesis. An epiclesis changes the Eucharist for Catholic orthodoxy by recasting an actual event into something other, in a different time and place. It also subjects the elements of the Mass to change and transformation. Epiclesis can, if taken to the extreme of its consequences, make the Mass, like art, into a similitude.

There was much to be gained, many possibilities offered, by Joyce's calling his stories "epicleti." An epiclesis is schismatic because, from the Catholic point of view in the liturgy of the Mass, it is a narrative of a previous event rather than the event itself. As such, it brings in its train all the effects of a narrative. It consists of a series of events related in the past tense, events of suggestion and provisionality rather than certainty. Such events have to be recalled by memory and reflection. Because provisional and because remembered only, the events so narrated have the status of a similitude, of something substituted metaphorically for what is supposed to be and otherwise considered actual.

In its challenge to Roman orthodoxy as a schismatic choice, epiclesis insists on a figurative event, not a literal one: thus, it is open to representation and mimesis. It is a dramatic representation rather than a real presence: therefore, it is a narrative account rather than an actual process. As a narrative, it evokes something of the past that requires memory and recall. It marks a movement of change and development. We shall see in the subsequent pages how much the *Dubliners* is affected by this intentionally provocative issue of "epicleti" and how much the stories are connected to Joyce's attraction to schism embodied in this term. It is also true that the parallel Joyce draws (as does Stephen) between the story and the Mass makes a possible metaphoric description for his art, because one consequence of epiclesis makes a figurative substitution in the Eucharist. Joyce does not merely use the word "epicleti" to impress and to posture (although he does that clearly in the letter to Curran); he uses it because it offers him a means to create an art free from the orthodoxy of his background and open to what he wishes to achieve.

"Epicleti" for Joyce is shorthand for a representational account of resemblance and a dramatic recounting of an act performed in some completed past that is recalled to memory by narrative. It marks a moment of change and transformation. In short, it describes the stories of the *Dubliners*, and it provides Joyce with the liberating power of a rupture from all that he has been taught. Joyce (seems) to have chosen to write "epicleti" as a way of getting free from orthodoxy in such a particular way as to be able to write his art. For Joyce, to be schismatic was to seize the necessary freedom to conceive of and carry out his own "calling," his summons of the spirit.

Because Joyce used the term in his letter to Curran unequivocally, whatever its mangled form, we need to examine the consequences of the schismatic epiclesis as a narrative and a dramatic account as Joyce would have encountered them, strange and liberating. We hope to be excused some fine points of theological and liturgical hairsplitting, as they clearly are things Joyce had been taught and told in catechism, and he would certainly have followed them to the uttermost with Jesuitical rigor as he tried to take a view of them askance.

The very first effect of naming his stories "epicleti" is to make what was orthodox in religion and even commonplace in narrative different and strange, to make art from another place and of another sort, even if its subject matter is the citizens of his native city. Joyce wishes to distinguish himself by rebellion from the orthodoxy of the past that he shared with Curran; he wished to distance himself from his background, his education, even the dogma of his country.

The dream of the boy in "The Sisters" introduces and grounds these issues of strangeness and the attractions of being contrary, or other, in confirmed misbelief: "I felt that I had been far away, in some land where the customs were strange, in Persia, I thought" (*D* 13–14). In addition to the distancing features of a repeated past time, "had been," and the act of attempted apprehension, "I thought" (two features to which we shall return below), it is strangeness that pervades the story in many ways, a glance to another place, standing off in differing apostasy.

If Joyce was nearly correct in misnaming "epicleti" to create an atmosphere of strangeness, the boy's vocabulary for his narration is deficient from the start. The strangeness of words is what initially confronts his thinking as he "passed the house," a familiar place, "night after night," an act he repeats, iteratively, in order to understand. He peers at the window in order to see a configuration of candles so that he can comprehend the effect, the "work," of paralysis. Of the words that sound "strangely" to his ears, "gnomon," we have observed, is possibly confused for "Gnostic" and is related etymologically to narrative (*gnaro*) as something imperfectly understood and therefore alien and transgressive: all in all, a schismatic movement associated with the far away of the East. In a similar "hiddenness," where a word is a cover, like an umbrella, for another word of sin and shame, Flynn's sister Eliza speaks of "rheumatic wheels" in a slip for "pneumatic." A hint of Gnosticism may emerge from the slip: those caught up with the spirit among Gnostics were called "pneumatikoi." Other faint gestures toward Eastern unorthodoxy can be glimpsed in the story, even in the uncle's jokingly calling the boy a "Rosicrucian," a member of shadowy sect that claims privileged knowledge from the Kabala and "Arabian magic" (*CE*, "Rosicrucian-ism" 12:193) and whose mother church is called the Holy Spirit, Pneuma Hagia (a name that will itself cast a long shadow into the *Wake* as we shall see). All strangeness from the East is schismatic and forbidden to Catholic orthodoxy.

The strangeness in the story is not only displaced far away "in some land" like Persia, it also resides in the presence in Dublin of the death of Father Flynn. Flynn's absence is a hovering presence in the story, not only as a corpse but as a figure in a dream, and the story alternately reveals and conceals the physical and the spiritual, the rational and the irrational, the natural and the supernatural. The epiclesis, in that it questions the transformation of elements in the Mass, is likewise an issue of presence and absence. "The Sisters" is a story of gesturing and figuring, of metaphoric and provisional attempts to connect with a real presence only dimly seen. The story raises the same questions as the Mass (it is a story about the mystery of the sacrament) that Joyce said was from the East and thus hidden and strange.

## 2

It would be difficult to state briefly an issue that has occupied church fathers for centuries. Catholic doctrine states that, in the consecration of the elements at the Mass, the words of Jesus at the Last Supper (of the bread, "This is my body"; of the wine, "This is my blood"), called the Institution, are sufficient alone to transform the bread and the wine into the actual body and blood of Christ; the elements are changed in their essentials, both bread and wine but also divine, the real presence of God. In this simple expression are two related and complicated facets of dogma. The Institution changes bread and wine in their substances, not their accidents (their external features), to the actual body and blood; this is the mystery of the transubstantiation. Joyce's fascination with this notion is not restricted to his early work: Stephen displays a continuing interest in this mystery in *Portrait* and *Ulysses* where it seems to be essential to his question of how to transform the real, a question for "the intellectual imagination." In transubstantiation, the elements become the divine, and thus the bread and wine are the Real Presence or God himself. Transubstantiation and the Real Presence, consequent one on the other, are crucial articles of faith for Catholic believers. This is the doctrine that Joyce would have been repeatedly taught in his student years. (On the issue of the elements, the Maynooth Catechism says, "Observing . . . that bread and wine are every day changed, by the power of nature, into human flesh and blood, we may more easily be led by this analogy to believe that the substance of the bread and wine is changed, by the celestial benediction, into the real flesh and blood of Christ"; on the Institution, "there is no room to doubt the reality of the flesh and blood of Christ.")[7] Moreover, Catholic dogma further states that it is the actual words of the Institution alone that make the Real Presence: it is "the literal sense of the words " and "not a figurative association," according the *Catholic Encyclopedia* ("Epiklesis," 5:503). Thus the words of the Institution are not a sign; the "is" in "This is my body" is not a copula. The Eucharistic Institution is literal and real, present and physical; it does not allow substitution or change; it is not metaphoric or figurative. Most pertinently, this orthodoxy states that the transubstantiation takes place immediately upon the words; it does not allow for the possibilities of recall and representation that Joyce found so congenial to his rebellious freedom in making art.

However, in the Mass of the Eastern Church (and it is the Eastern Church with which Joyce associates "The Sisters,") there follows the words of the Institution a request to the Holy Spirit to transform the elements into the body and the blood of Christ. This is the epiclesis and it has three very particular effects that we shall discuss at length: that there is a narrative created in the Mass; how that narrative is constructed in time and thus remembered and recalled; and finally (more distantly from the Greek Church) there is the effect of how that narrative in one heretical version becomes a similitude and a metaphor. All these are pertinent to Joyce's art, in its first appearances and its last expressions, signaled by Joyce's schismatic turn in the very deliberate if misnamed use of "epicleti."

The point of the Western orthodox claim against the East is that this invocation by the epiclesis has the effect of diminishing the Institution itself into a description of the Last Supper rather than a transformative and ongoing moment in and of itself. Instead of the nearly simultaneous way in which the Institution in Catholic doctrine timelessly connects the current Eucharist with the Crucifixion, the present altar with the Last Supper table, the epiclesis of the Eastern Church has the effect (according to Catholic interpretation) of making the words and the actions of the Mass ("took bread, broke it, and said") into an event that has come to an end in the past, an event not ongoing in the present. For Catholic dogma, the epiclesis thus turns the Institution, in the words of the *Catholic Encyclopedia*, into "a narrative," making the scene unfold as if it were a description rather than an actual action (5:503). The interpretation of the Catholic Eucharist is logically connected to the orthodox metaphysics of the Real Presence: the event of the Last Supper, even while having taken place in the past, is however an ongoing action, eternally in heaven and continuously at every Mass, due to its divine performance. (The Butler Catechism has it that Jesus "continues to offer himself" in the Mass [49]; similarly another widespread catechism of the nineteenth century, Deharbe, puts it as "the perpetual sacrifice of the New Law" [267]). A commentary on the Eucharist notes: "It is the very nature of the Christian liturgy of the Mass that the account of the Institution of the Blessed Sacrament should not be recited as a merely *historical* record. . . . Indeed the words are spoken over the bread and chalice."[8] The Greek Mass, because of the epiclesis, changes that assumption. In one commentary (1912) nearly contemporary with Joyce's religious instruction, Father Adrian Fortescue, notes that the epiclesis comes after the Institution, so that these connections cannot obtain (307). Thus, "it is impossible to understand the text as a merely *historic* statement, in the way demanded by the [Eastern] rubric at this point" (336, emphasis added). Roman orthodoxy rejects the notion of a history, something both in the past and subject to a recounting, and this was the orthodoxy Joyce would have been taught about the consequences of the epiclesis.

History and narrative therefore come about by a contrarian stance because of the epiclesis; they are the provenance of art as much as of religion. Catholic dogma, as expressed in the entry in the *Catholic Encyclopedia* on "Epiklesis," asserts that the claim of narrative comes from the official Euchologion of the Eastern Church that states: "therefore the words of the Lord are repeated as a narrative [*diegematikos*]"(5:503). The Catholic charge against a "historical record" reflects the etymology of the Greek *diegematikos* as a narrative whose particular task is related to knowledge of the events recounted in a history. Both history and narrative have as their roots words meaning to know or understand: one of them, history, is related to the verb "to see" (εἴδω, Latin *video*); the other, the narrative, to the knowledge that also makes the word *gnomon* (γνοέω, Latin *gnaro, narrare*). The consequence of this effect of the epiclesis as retelling, in the orthodox Catholic view, is thus that the Last Supper mentioned in the Mass with an epiclesis thus becomes a scene, "nothing but a dramatic representation" and not an actual event; in fact it is said to take place "in a succession of time"(*CE* 5:503). In short, from the definition provided by the Catholic encyclopedia's doctrinal position, one might say that the epiclesis makes the Last Supper into a brief story, a work of narrative representation. This claim is certainly what Joyce was taught, and the Greek error must have had a large attraction. Joyce must have felt that the church was keeping him from knowing and telling, much as the boy in the story "The Sisters" feels excluded from the meaning of events. The knowing recitation of an earlier event and the narration of a dramatized scene are schismatic consequences for the Roman Church, but they are very appealing possibilities for stories. Epiclesis as a schismatic notion is transgressive; as a literary idea it is an artistic possibility opened by that rupture. For these reasons Joyce calls his stories "epicleti."

By pursuing the relationship between a Eucharistic and a schismatic, dramatic narrative with the rigor of logical (even Jesuitical) thinking, we arrive at the next major consequence of the Mass that is also a model for Joyce's stories: the fact that as an act of narrative the Mass takes place in the past. Thus every schismatic rite is an act of memory commemorating the event, with the Eucharist being a recall of a completed act. Although less so in the Greek ritual, the notion of the Eucharist as an event recalled from the past and remembered in time is very strong in the later Protestant schismatic deviation from the Catholic rite. As a retrospective arrangement, a schismatic Eucharist resembles the post hoc description of fictional narrative forms. As the past act is to be available to and accessible by recollection, the narrative's act of memory is a recounting. Such retelling in the past tense is an art form.

To see how an epiclesis makes the Eucharist a remembered event narrated in the past and how the Greek epiclesis is further developed by the Protestant, and second, schism in the Anglican Mass (the Protestant service closest to the Catholic, although renegade from it), it is necessary to delve into the precise way the Institution of the Last Supper is presented in the liturgies.

If the epiclesis makes the Greek Mass a "historical," reported narrative account, Jesus' actions at the Last Supper in the Eucharist of both the Greek and Latin masses are, however identical, conveyed in the past tense.[9] The Latin and Greek mass employ the simple past tense for Jesus' actions at the Last Supper: "he took, broke, and gave." The perfect tense in Latin and the aorist in Greek are tenses that more clearly indicate an action completed in the past than the English past tense.[10] There are similarly in both masses imperatives understood to be spoken in the past: "take," "eat," "drink." The admonitory actions—"giving thanks" to God, "saying" to the disciples—appear in the participial form in both languages, a form less determinant in time than is, for example, the simple past.[11] In other words, the use of the present form with the past tense indicates an action in the same tense as the main verbs (the simple past), but the effect of the present participle is open to the residual sense of being an action in the present or continuing into the present.

The effect of the participles ("giving" and "saying") is to suggest through the indeterminacy of the grammar that there is a residual present tense to those actions consistent with the Catholic view of the Eucharist as an ongoing, eternal action. From a chronological point of view, giving thanks and saying are actions performed in the past time of the Last Supper; but from the theological and orthodox point of view (and this is the powerful and perplexing part of the Eucharist that Joyce seemed to acknowledge when he would not take a perfunctory communion), these actions of gratitude and admonition are constant, present, and perpetual acts once upon a time in Palestine and now at every moment of the Mass: that is what the orthodox belief in the real presence of God means in the Catholic Mass.

The fact that the epiclesis Joyce singles out comes, in the Greek Mass, after the Institution, means that the account regardless of its tenses is just a descriptive act. Surely that fact appeals heavily to Joyce, because narrative acts are what make his art. His words create and represent, much as the divine word makes and presents; he can claim for himself his own sort of artistic Institution. In order to more clearly see this point, however, it is necessary to establish how the Protestant Mass further extends the concept of the remembered past time in the effects derived from a schismatic dramatic narrative. To do so, it is necessary to look closely at the tenses in the Anglican Mass, the other schismatic mass, because there the effect is most clearly seen.

If Joyce was not familiar with the Greek liturgy until Trieste, he had enough knowledge of Anglican worship to refer to the Book of Common Prayer in *Hero* in 1905—a fact we will explore to other purposes in the next chapter.[12] He may also have been familiar with the different prayer book from orthodox catechetical instruction.[13] The Anglican prayer book of Joyce's university years was identical to the 1662 book. With the exception of certain prayers, the prayer book of the Church of Ireland even after the disestablishment was identical to the 1662 book. In all, there is strong reason to presume that Joyce would have been lightly familiar with the Anglican rite and its disposition toward the narrative sequence in time when he used the term "epicleti" as he planned his stories.

The Anglican Mass in Cranmer's translations of the Latin continues with the notion of a narrative but adds two other dimensions: the first, or grammatical, dimension is a refinement of the tenses of the "represented" Last Supper; the second or heterodoxically doctrinal, dimension holds that the elements at the Eucharist are not transubstantiated but consubstantiated, and that principle, along with the remembered narrative, creates a simulacrum and a metaphor, a fully Protestant notion, heretical to Rome and the East both. A studied heresy with narrative and metaphoric dimensions: is it any wonder that Joyce would be so attracted to the notion of epiclesis as a schismatic term that would further his attempts at art?

The Anglican Mass of Cranmer is like the Greek in that it is a narrative, but it becomes so not because of an epiclesis but because it treats the chronology of the Institution itself by using different tenses, and that difference is what may appeal to Joyce in bringing both Greek and Anglican schismatic gestures together in the English language.[14] In his native tongue Joyce can have the rebellious appeal of using the vernacular against the Latin Mass.

Cranmer's translation of the liturgy clearly tracks the *Missale romanum*, but his emphasis on the time frame of the Institution is different.[15] The 1662 Book of Common Prayer is the clearest point of reference, because it provides a convenient overview of the different time sequences attendant on the theological and liturgical differences of the Latin and then the heretical Eucharist. By contrast with the Latin and Greek masses, with their simple past tense and indeterminate participles, Cranmer's English liturgy clearly indicates events that take place in a past of two time frames by reference to two past tenses, not just the simple past. In the Institution's same order of actions and tenses as in the Latin and Greek masses, Cranmer places the actions of Jesus at the Cenacle in the simple past: "took bread . . . brake it and gave it (worthy of note is the simple past of "break," now obsolete). Along with actions cast in simple past tense, Cranmer also has the imperatives "take, eat" and the participle form "saying" to introduce those commands, indeterminate in time but again understood to be contemporaneous with "brake" and "gave." Yet the attendant action of giving thanks—expressed in the Latin and Greek masses with a present participle that reflects the past with a residual effect of ongoing, present action—is unequivocally rendered by Cranmer with an active verb in the past perfect tense and further temporally located by an adverb as an act occurring prior to the past actions: "When he had given thanks, He took bread and brake it." The foremost effect of this construction is to locate the action of thanks as completed even further back, earlier in a clear sequence of causality and temporality, before the bread is broken and given. It creates an unmistakably delineated series of acts extending backward, an effect repeated in the treatment of the wine: "after he had blessed, he took, saying." So the Anglican Eucharist, most pertinently schismatic to Catholicism because of the consubstantiation which to orthodoxy was only a similitude, is further alien because of its chronology: it is an event taking place solely within the past, both simple and compound. Thus the Anglican Mass actually enacts the Catholic claim of the Greek rite being a narrative. Through the clear use of nested tenses, Cranmer's version clearly is a narrative. While the reasons for this are theological, directly related to the Protestant firm belief that the events of the Last Supper are a recalled commemoration and not the Real Presence of an ongoing time, the events are clearly indicated as taking place within the past recaptured in successive events performed in a sequence of past times—the tenses of, as it were, a narrative act. Its sequence of time as completed and connected leads Catholic dogma to

teach it as schismatic and a narrative: it is not, as the Catholics believe and create in the liturgy, an ongoing presence eternally the past and continuously the
present, but rather a related sequence of actions performed and then related
and remembered in the liturgy. That is the sort of narrative Joyce seeks for the
*Dubliners.* The stories of the *Dubliners* are similarly narrated as events taking
place in two pasts in regression, with the narrative occurring in the immediate
past of the narrator and the memory of a more distant past in which the actions
performed took place in the past perfect before being narrated in the simple
past of the narrator in the act of narrating.

While it would be too much to suggest that the tenses and time frame of the
*Dubliners* is due precisely to that wording in Cranmer's liturgy or that Joyce
would have had any need to go to the Eucharist for instruction in narrative,
there is a connection and appeal of narrative derived from the possibilities of
schism in describing the stories "epicleti"; it is worth remarking that the opening of "The Sisters" (that story compared to the schismatic Greek Mass) cap-
tures the sense of past event taking place within a frame of receding, repeated
acts: "There was no hope for him this time: it was the third stroke. Night after
night I had passed the window (it was vacation time) and studied the lighted
square of the window: and night after night I had found it lighted the same
way. . . . If he was dead, I thought, I would see the reflection of candles on the
darkened blind for I knew that two candles must be set at the head of a corpse"
(*D* 9). Particularly striking is the repeated act of the past of the pluperfect,
"I had passed . . . I had found," along with the past of a completed action, "I
passed" and "I studied." There is inference, "I knew," based on a conditional
past perfect: "if he was dead, I would see." All this is an enactment of the drama
inherent in a narrative account reflective of past events connected in time,
and it is just like the effect of the schismatic Greek and Protestant Masses. It is
pertinent to emphasize three keys words in this attempt at narrative recall: "I
*thought* I would *see* . . . for I *knew.*" The Greek narrative of the Eucharist was
rejected by Catholic orthodoxy because of its being a *diegematikos*—a historical and narrative form related etymologically to "seeing" and to "knowing." The
etymology of "gnomon" and "paralysis" in the opening pages of the story also
indicate why Joyce called the stories "epicleti"—because he longs to see, like
"paralysis," that schismatic move of epiclesis at work.

The way in which Joyce intended epiclesis to describe the schismatic Mass
as an event narrated and remembered is most evidently seen in the story's being a retelling of an earlier event, remembered. Time is a crucial element in the
first three stories in *Dubliners* as the narrators try unsuccessfully as adults to
describe their incompletely understood actions as children. In "The Sisters,"
this distance between the narrator and the boy is signaled by the word "inef-

ficacious," one that would be an unlikely choice by the young boy to whom the word "paralysis" sounds strange. Most pertinent to our purposes and most interesting, "efficacious" is a word originally used to describe the effective working of the divine: the *New English Dictionary* (1897)[16] cites its first usage from 1528 in "Goddis worde is so efficacious." The story is, conversely, about failed efficacy.

The story is a narration of an earlier event, the death of Flynn, which takes place within a past of repeated acts, both iterative and aorist: "night after night I passed . . . and I studied." Within that repeated past, the narration seeks a more present attempt to uncover the meaning of events that have already occurred. The activity of recovering umbrellas as the "work" of the Flynn sisters only reproduces the effect in the narration of trying to recover and capture meaning, and the obscurity and confusion of what is covered (the little shade of "umbrella") recalls the hiddenness that Joyce saw in the Greek Mass. Most importantly, the attempt to narrate (from Latin *gnaro* [acquainted with], derived from *gnoscere*) is an attempt to tell in such a way as to have the authority of seeming to know (and the verb to know is related, as we know from looking at the Latin and Greek Mass, to *gnoscere* in Latin, and to γνοέω in Greek). The perplexing and occluded word "gnomon," placed at the very start of the story, is thus surely an indication (to Joyce, but not to the boy) of a vital connection. It is unequivocally related etymologically to the act of narration upon which both Joyce and the boy place such emphasis; the narrative is thus like Gnosticism, a schismatic act, as is the "epicleti" of "The Sisters" itself. The mystery in the story is the mystery of the dramatized narration of a past and imperfectly remembered event; it is an act of schismatic possibility.

The schismatic Eucharist is a commemoration of the Last Supper: not a perpetual and ongoing event but a remembrance of it. The story is similarly concerned with acts of commemoration within a fraught time sequence of the past and the pluperfect. The boy's association with the strangeness of the East comes about because of his attempt "to remember what happened afterwards in the dream" (*D* 13). This attempt is twice bundled in time: trying to remember an elusive event, a dream, and then sequentially trying to construct the order of what happened in its past. The first thing the boy remembers is a lamp, a sign of illumination which reflects his attempt to find meaning in the position of the candle lights in the death room with which the story begins. He finds he cannot "remember" the last part of the dream, "the end."

The complicated time frame of the story is evident, as the sequence of past times, simple and complex, is jumbled. The later part of that dream is the first remembered, when his "soul receded into a pleasant and vicious region" (presumably that of the East) where he finds "the face of the paralytic" waiting for him to confess. The boy catches himself up to free himself from the night-mare: "then I remembered that it too had died of paralysis." Through an act of memory, the boy tries to free himself from being trapped by the demands of his religious mentor. The dream is said to occur after the evening in which Cotter brings the news of Flynn's death and speaks "the unfinished sentences" from which the boy tries to "puzzle his head to extract the meaning." At that time, he had not yet visited the shop nor attended the death bed. The detail of the "grey heavy face of the paralytic" that appears in the dream is actually from his later, subsequent experience while attending the corpse of the priest laid out (retold at the conclusion of the story). The sequence of the narration has been altered by the adult narrator's collapsing the time of an immediate and distant past, just as the commemorative Eucharist is said to do. In the same way, the "pleasant and vicious" region first remembered in the dream is later described as "somewhere where customs are strange"; but surely the boy proceeds post hoc, the place coming after the qualities associated with it, rather than in logi-cal sequence: first place, then its features. His belatedness resembles Joyce's later adoption of previous schismatic positions. The same conditional quality to his interpretative retelling is suggested by a sentence hedged with conditions such as this: "had he not been dead I would have gone."

Acts of memory are not confined to the questioning boy and the telling narrator. The bereaved Eliza is aware of temporal changes: "I won't be bring-ing him his beef-tea any more," where the description of her repeated act, the iterative past, will not be continued into the future. She is said, with this reflec-tion, to be "communing with the past." "Communion" as conversing with the nonpresent dead (with its slight touch of spiritualism) gives way in importance to "communion" as the Eucharist itself, which through epiclesis is a schismatic enactment of a prior and then remembered event, which now lacks any Real Presence, just as Eliza now lacks a brother.

Many other stories in *Dubliners* similarly attempt to explain past events, so that they are narratives of completed actions that justify Joyce's schismatic choice to call them "epicleti" of a Mass. It is worth remarking that of all of Joyce's works *Dubliners* is the one which is most directly narrated in the com-pound past tense. The indirect narrative of *Portrait* and the interior monologue of *Ulysses* are immediate rather than mediated forms, presenting material di-rectly. The *Wake* has a narrative which, as the past tense, is constantly open to repeated and ongoing access. *Dubliners* is rather a narratively recovered past. The stories in *Dubliners* attempt explanations of obscure events, hidden from their narrators who are nonetheless present at those events. If all stories contain an epiphany, as many critics have argued, it is because they seek to illuminate something hidden away in obscurity through narration; what is hidden is some spiritual meaning like the spirit of efficaciousness invoked by the epiclesis.

The first stories of *Dubliners* evince the strongest working of this impulse to narrate an event located in the distant past using simple past tense, as in each an older narrator recounts earlier events. Most interesting in this regard is that while the first three stories in the collection as published—or "intended" (to use Joyce's term to Curran)—all have this strong retrospective narration where an older narrator recounts obscure events surrounding a younger self, the dates of composition vary: "The Sisters," 1904, revised 1906; "An Encounter," 1905; and "Araby," 1905. This fact argues that Joyce's intent to reproduce the commemorative narration consequent on his making the stories "epicleti" obtains over a nearly three-year span of writing. When assembling his stories, Joyce seems to have foregrounded those three which most do the work of remembrance and recounting, so that his claim to be writing "epicleti" is made evident at the outset of the collection. When the boy at the end of "An Encounter" notes of Mahoney that "I had always despised him a little," the features of the iterative past and the pluperfect call back the intricate time sequence of present memory and a repeated past. Similarly, "The Boarding House" (the fifth story composed, in 1905)—although part of another thematic sequence of stories of adolescence—ends with Polly's daydreaming, an occurrence that seeks to account for an earlier, continuing action:"Then she remembered what she had been waiting for," a series of acts of compressed passed time and memory like the boy's dream in "The Sisters." Even the late story, "The Dead," whose composition is a new direction as much as a coda to the collection, has crucial elements of memory: Gretta's past forced upon Gabriel transforms the substance of her presence in his life. Another strong connection among those first three stories written over a long time frame is that they also continue with the idea of Eastern strangeness that Joyce first noted with reference to the Greek Mass and "The Sisters." The strange man in "An Encounter" whose green eyes are a sign of his being foreign calls up the alienating character of "abroad," and his strange advances resemble those of the figure in the boy's dream of Father Flynn. The "eastern enchantment" of the syllables in the name "Araby" charm the boy in that story with a spell of heroic and liberating adventure, much as the epiclesis Joyce invokes in writing his stories betokens another attraction of the East as schismatic possibility.

Thus, Joyce's invocation of "epicleti" in 1904 to describe his stories before he writes and publishes them in 1905 (and beyond) carries a promise that, in breaking with the orthodoxy of his youth, he can attain a precipitate that makes his stories into art, an art schismatic at its center. In his offhand comment to

Curran, Joyce seems to make a connection between the brief moments in his stories and the transformative power of fiction. He drives an albeit oblique connection that both animates his work and gives a body to his written word. Because epiclesis is doctrinally unsound, it was appealing in and of itself to Joyce, and, moreover, could do much for his art.

Before proceeding, we should consider one additional feature of the schismatic Mass changed by epiclesis into narrative and further challenged by the Protestant version of recall. It is conducive to Joyce's purposes because it gets to the very nature of representation and is essential to the notion of epiclesis as the possibility for art: for a schismatic Protestant Mass, now two steps removed by rupture from Catholic orthodoxy, the elements of the Mass are a figuration, a similitude. While both the Latin and Greek hold that the moment of consecration varies within the Eucharist—the Latin at the words of the Institution, the Greek after the epiclesis, on the important point of the status of the bread and wine both agree that the elements are transubstantiated (μεταουσις in Greek). It is the Protestant view—where bread and wine *are* the divine by similitude—that imparts rebellious rigor to Joyce's sense of art as metonymic in its transformations. It is in this opening made by schism that the long-held parallel of the Mass to art is made possible at all, as a source of the metaphor that sustains much of Joyce's descriptions of his art.

Returning to Catholic doctrine (for Joyce must always start there to turn away), the words of the Last Supper—the actual words, not figurative associations—institute the Real Presence; the result is the transubstantiated elements. The Eastern Church also believes that the elements are subject to such essential change, even if the epiclesis is required. By contrast, the Reformation churches in the second great schism from Rome did not assent to the Real Presence nor to transubstantiation. So again, with the term epiclesis, Joyce evokes the spirit of apostasy: not only the difference between the Roman and Eastern churches (the first schism), but also that within the Western churches (the second great split in the Church Universal). At the Reformation, the debate surrounding the Institution centered on treating the words not as literal (the Roman position) but rather as representational.[17] Luther himself believed that the words of the Institution were literal and believed as well in consubstantiation rather than transubstantiation. (Luther, we will see, hovers over Joyce's use of the vernacular Bible in the next chapter.) The so-named sacramentalist position was nuanced, reflecting all the various differences set loose by Luther's challenge to Roman authority in this as in all matters. However, what all the sacramentalists had in common was the belief that the word at the Last Supper ("this is my body" "this is my blood") were not literal. Ulrich Zwingli considered the "is" in "this is my body" a "copula," thus insisting on a figurative association.

(Johannes Oecolampadius considered the words a *signum* or *figura*). To invoke epiclesis is then to assert the representational, figurative quality of divine creation and sacrifice; and creation and sacrifice for Joyce are the necessary actions in making his art.

The issue allows Joyce to engage difference within difference, schism within schism. Not only is epiclesis not Roman, and thus schismatic at its origin, it is also something which has caused difference within the Protestant churches and even with the Anglican one. The finer threads of schism appeal to Joyce, as do any challenges to unitary meaning: his interest always peaks when any authority is challenged from within. So for Joyce to consider the epiclesis was not only to separate from Rome by gesturing toward the Eastern Church, but also to glance at the tensions within the various and not uniform Protestant ones. Joyce (as we shall see in chapter 5) was always interested in schism because it allowed for a break from a dominant power into local choice and freedom.

It was Cranmer, that source of the Mass narrative built around carefully sequenced English past and pluperfect tenses, who stated—in a phrasing as much like Shakespeare on his artistic semiology as like Cranmer himself on the Eucharist—that the elements are "the outward and visible sign of an inward and spiritual grace," allowing for the Zwinglian possibility of substitution. Orthodox Catholicism acknowledges the first part of Cranmer's formulation: the Butler Catechism states that the sacraments are "a visible, that is outward sign of action." Butler notes dogmatically, however, that they are "instituted by Christ" in time and are therefore continuous as the Real Presence (45). Thus, the Anglican Mass considers the elements as a similitude, something not actually present but suggested. If epiclesis in the Eastern Church of the first schism made the Institution a narrative, that narrative account is developed further by the Protestant and Anglican churches of the second schism, which made the elements into something that shows forth, something within a metaphoric relationship between sign and meaning, sign and wonder. It is something that seeks to bridge inner world with outer, physical world with spiritual, both designated and ineffable. So epiclesis seems not only to be like Joyce's epiphanies, it is suggestively like art. The mysterious workings of the divine as well as of meaning are suggested by epiclesis; the reference to the hiddenness of the Greek Mass in Joyce's letter of 1906 and many of Joyce's early stories are about the mysterious workings of meaning hidden from the narrators.

The particular consequences of the word choice "epiclesis," associated with figuration and signs and representing intellectually complex challenges to doctrine, were important to Joyce, so that his art becomes schismatic at its inception. Therefore, by designating the stories of *Dubliners* "epicleti," Joyce foregrounded several intricate and well-thought out comparisons consistent with his schismatic views dating to the beginning of his career. We have discussed the narrative and dramatic implications of the term with reference to verb tense and narrative recollection. Here we see what the term does for the notion of representation. A narrative Eucharist, which allows the possibility that the elements in the Mass may not be the actual body and blood but rather a similitude and figuration is clearly something that already functions *as* art. In *My Brother's Keeper*, Stanislaus recounts a conversation with his brother in the Dublin streets that has all the elements of a peripatetic theological debate in its metaphysical speculation and refutation. It takes place in 1904, the year of Joyce's "epicleti" letter and of the first of his *Dubliners* stories. This actual conversation contains some of the seeds of Joyce's art: it is the source of events in fiction, replayed in *Portrait* between Stephen and Lynch. Art and theology run parallel in the dialogue between the brothers. Stanislaus tells Jim that he will not take communion at Easter—a stance Joyce fictionalized as Stephen's own in *Portrait*. In a fashion true to their scholastic training with the Jesuits, the brothers start with the issue of what happens in the Mass that Stanislaus refuses, that doctrine of the Real Presence in the transformed elements: "You mean that you don't believe in transubstantiation, said Jim with ironical emphasis on the polysyllable."[18] While Joyce may want to challenge his brother's faith and knowledge, the irony of his emphasis is aimed at the notion of transubstantiation itself as something less than it claims. The "Real Presence" of orthodoxy is a term which immediately—and logically—on its face obviates the possibility of metaphoric substitution; it does not allow for anything other than itself.

To have a freedom, Joyce must have something else, something schismatic. The theological issue now raised, Joyce turns the conversation away from Stanislaus (and characteristically) to himself and to his art while retaining something of the gravity and importance of the sacraments (whose issues for him are synonymous with the Mass). He pursues the notion of his art as something consubstantial and figurative: "there is a certain resemblance between the mystery of the Mass and what I am trying to do. I mean that I am trying . . . to give people some kind of intellectual pleasure or spiritual enjoyment by converting the bread of everyday life into something that has permanent artistic life of its own . . . for their mental, moral, and spiritual uplift, he concluded glibly."[19] What Stanislaus persistently sees as a humorous exchange, ironical and glib, retains a certain intellectual depth and weight. Its connection to matters raised by a schismatic Mass, signaled by Joyce's use of the term "epicleti" in his letter to Curran, is reinforced in this exchange because Joyce refers yet again to the issue of "resemblance," a term that for a Catholic is completely heterodox. (We can draw from this conversation a thread that links it to his story "The

Sisters," in turn tied to the schismatic Greek Mass.) Joyce goes on to declare to Stanislaus that the "The Mass on Good Friday seems to me a very great drama." That Mass has no Eucharist, as the sacraments are supplied from the reserve; the service enacts the space of the empty tomb until Eastern Sunday. As such, it has a highly performative aspect that Joyce acknowledges when he notes its drama. Much as with the epiphany as narrative, the Good Friday Mass as drama highlights the literary qualities that Joyce wished to develop through displaced liturgical ones. He embraces what orthodoxy shuns, the Mass as a schismatic representational art form. When Joyce follows an idea in the power of his intellectual and rebellious imagination, he remains consistent and thorough. He continues with the idea of a schismatic, rather than a Catholic Eucharist: The Mass when it has an epiclesis as in the Greek rite is a drama; when it is Protestant, it is a figuration.

By adopting the schismatic consequences of a religion that promulgates similitude, Joyce conceives of religion as metaphor, religion as *like* art. In order even to make the claim that art is a resemblance, he must see orthodoxy greatly askance. Joyce claims he is giving people "intellectual pleasure and spiritual enjoyment," and if he is glib, he is also honest: it is he who finds intellectual pleasure in making the ideas of the church into challenges and choices; whose schismatic turn, in stories that adapt an epiclesis to make drama and narrative memory, provides him enjoyment of spiritual properties.

Perhaps the most overt pronouncement Joyce made about his art and religion occurs in this exchange with Stanislaus: that he is "converting the bread of everyday life into something that has a permanent artistic life." This is a concept that, unlike "epicleti," is widely remembered, but it serves the same purpose. It is clearly an idea that owes its impulse to many sources: the classical view of art as something beyond the effects of time and as a tribute to the power of the artist. The claim so phrased, however, clearly owes its meaning to questions of Eucharistic transubstantiation that the brothers argue about at the beginning of their conversation. Religion is certainly at the center of this conception of art. Yet at the very center of the parallel of art and religion is something schismatic.

At this juncture we must revisit two old chestnuts about Joyce and religion, long-held critical ideas that need to be rethought in a discussion of Joyce's willfully schismatic moves. There is first the easy way Scholes pursues the analogy of art to the Mass while thereby obscuring the schismatic nature of this parallel: "As Joyce explained to his brother Stanislaus, 'there is a certain resemblance between the mystery of the mass.'"[20] Scholes assumes an analogy here, but does not acknowledge the intellectual challenge Joyce intends with this very Protestant notion of similitude; it is fundamental to the logic of the claim that the

Mass *can be* a resemblance. Joyce bases his conception of art as religion on the schismatic premises of the religion that promulgates ideas of similitude.

This institutional sentence by Joyce ("there is a certain resemblance"), where he turns religion into art is the source from which Ellmann derives his famous pronouncement, "Christianity evolved [in Joyce's mind] from a religion into a system of metaphors."[21] Ellmann's claim appears valid, but it is so not because of Joyce's anticlericalism nor because of his rejection of religion. Ellmann considers Joyce's abandonment of religion a good thing: the word "evolved" betrays, of course, the secular view that Joyce moved on to more complicated ideas than those found in religion. But the truth behind Ellmann's statement comes not from Joyce's abandonment of religion but from his rigorous thinking about the nature of unorthodoxy and rebellious rupture. Ellmann waxes metaphoric in his claim that Joyce "converted the temple to new uses instead of trying to knock it down." Joyce was no Samson, nor was he, despite his own sense of martyrdom, like Christ. He did not convert the temple but rather subverted the proprietorship of its head priests; this religious demesne could be held by others with very good, if challenging, claims to its space. Ellmann is too universal in his claim. It is not "Christianity" that evolves for Joyce but rather orthodox Roman Catholic doctrine. Joyce would not believe that Rome possessed a firm lease on sacred space and sought other claimants. For Joyce, to evoke the intellectual consequences of the theology of the Mass by naming his works for the epiclesis of the Eastern Church and to call them, with recourse to Protestant terminology, a "resemblance," was hardly to reject Christianity, but rather to embrace the challenge to Rome's exclusive claim to that metaphoric temple.

While Stanislaus' diary of 1904 contains Joyce's idea of art in metaphoric relationship to religion, that idea persists well into *Portrait*. There, Stephen makes the famous pronouncement of his intent to "transmut[e] the daily bread of experience into the radiant body of ever living life" (*P* 221). This claim obviously has analogs in classical notions of art as eternal. It also stresses Joyce's conviction that mimesis is essential to art that, in turn, resembles nature; art needs a quotidian subject. Yet the sentence continues Joyce's association of art with religious ideas. Easily taken as simple analogy, this declaration is rarely examined for its radically schismatic underpinnings. The verb "transmute" is a claim of power for art that stands in complete contradistinction to the Roman view of what occurs to the elements of the Mass as transubstantiated: the bread and wine changed into the body and blood retain their original appearance and form, while elements "transmuted" would be changed utterly—in form as well as in function. Stephen's claim for art is by no means an easy equivalence, nor is it an orthodox position; transmutation hovers at the edge of the illicit and the alien. Moreover, his declaration not only treats religion as a metaphor, but also makes the power of art the power of metaphor: art itself changes elements by a sort of alchemy (the verb "transmute" falls, of course, within the nomenclature of the mysterious science), and those changes are ones of figuration and metonymy.[22] Art is not only a similitude of life, but also of a sacrament.

Joyce not only challenges the late nineteenth-century Catholic Church in its authority, but also questions some of the pieties of modernism by his association of religion and art. Because the epiclesis, from Roman orthodoxy, renders the Mass's transubstantiational Eucharistic moment into a figuration, into something representational, the schismatic rupture that drives Joyce's thinking about religion and art enables him to treat religion and metaphor as the same thing, not as substitutes one for the other. The Eucharist in particular, but all religious gestures, emblems, and stories in their "transcendence" are signifiers of all signifiers. In a strikingly different sort of apostasy, Joyce's texts preview and inadvertently challenge poststructuralist dogma about the substance of language. In a postmodernist reading of Aquinas, two philosophers, John Milbank and Catherine Pickstock, argue an anti-Derridean view of the Eucharist, in which the absence of the referent cannot be true of the Mass because the Institution insists that the referent for the bread, "this is my body," is present and specific. Thus the conjointure of bread and divine body are conformed in "ontological coincidence" (93). They point out the Protestant difference with their interpretation of Catholic orthodoxy, noting that in the Calvinist view the Institution's "this" is "intended metaphorically," which is the position that Joyce seeks to hold (89). The authors go on to note that, if the Aquinian rejection of Derrida's view is itself rejected, the "Eucharistic signs perforce become . . . a matter of non-essential *illustrative* signification, which relies upon a . . . conventional (if mimetic) similitude of bread and Body, and the wine and the blood"—which again comes to what Joyce seeks to assert in contrast to orthodoxy (93). So, in seeing the Mass as a similitude, Joyce at one and the same time rejects Catholic orthodoxy and rejects, proleptically, the postmodernist assumption that all language is multireferential. One could say Joyce insists on epiclesis so that he can (1) logically assert that his art is religious and (2) that both art and religion are metaphors; to do so would be both consistent and schismatic with the orthodox beliefs of the nineteenth-century religious community, as well as with those of a postmodernist orthodoxy of the literary-critical community in the twentieth. Mimesis, as defined by Aristotle, is an early interest of Joyce's from the Pola notebook and important to his art. Mimesis is also crucial to his schismatic turn as he replays and replicates the positions of famous heresies.

Yet the issue of the epiclesis is compounded even beyond representational limits because, even when successful, the Eucharistic request invokes a mystery. There, elements must be transformed by the agency of the Holy Spirit—an act provisional at a time indeterminate. What Joyce claims for his stories as for the Mass is such a sense of rite or puzzle, something obscure and not readily apparent. Mystery involves something secret, something that involves shutting the eyes (or lips) in a process performed by ritual—be that ritual the sacrament or the writing. Mystery has a physical component (the ritual, the gestures) and also a spiritual one (obscurity and occlusion). Religion and art both have at their core, their heart, a power of wonder, what Joyce calls in his 1904 exchange with Stanislaus an intellectual pleasure and spiritual enjoyment. Both seek to grasp a barely accessible, if equal, inward meaning from outward signs.

"The Sisters" attempts to understand what seems to motivate all visible actions, what purposes lie behind the "working" of events understood by means of words—as when the boy tries to "extract meaning from unfinished sentences" spoken by adults or from "books as thick as the Post Office Directory" "written by the fathers of the Church" (D 13). Indeed a narrative of naturalistic detail (indeed, all narrative) is just such an attempt to understand the outward side of things. Attempting to read visual clues—the positions of the candles in the window of the death room—is an effort to find what is hidden from the surface, what seems elusive, mysterious. Thus the entire narrative remembered as the past becomes an effort, only partially efficacious, to see the spiritual in signs. Here the epiclesis as a feature from the schismatic Anglican Mass comes back into play. It is of course the spirit which is invoked by the epiclesis in the Eucharist, a request to the Holy Ghost to sanctify the elements. Joyce uses to great effect in "The Sisters" two unorthodox freedoms: one achieved in his schismatic move to the strangeness of the Greek Mass and the other through the figurative powers of the Mass's Anglican consubstantiation. "The Sisters" is replete with a heterodox search for meaning, a request for understanding. The signs must be read, if only imperfectly and with much the same provisionality as the epiclesis which, despite its evocation of the spirit, may not effect any transformation of the elements. As Father Flynn discovered when he dropped the chalice, there may be nothing there.

The uneven and desultory religious instruction the boy receives from Flynn seems to circle around questionable schismatic issues, imperfectly remembered and inadequately understood. Flynn teaches the boy to pronounce Latin properly, but the Greek of "simony" and "gnomon" are beyond him. The boy claims to have learned the meaning of the different ceremonies of the Mass and of the different vestments worn by the priest, but this combination of spiritual matters and visible figures escapes him. He learns the responses to the Mass so that he can participate in the ceremony, combining as best he can the physical signs of the Mass with the spiritual meaning that lies occluded behind it. His "patter" (*D* 13) of rote responses suggests empty action, much as the word "patter" as a reflective response comes from a corruption of the Our Father (Pater Noster). By performing the role of the acolyte when Flynn does not actually celebrate a Mass, the boy skirts dangerously near a replay of the traumatic moment of Flynn's priesthood, when another boy, the acolyte, dropped the chalice. Repetition here of empty gestures is a sort of compulsion.

The boy considers the simplest physical acts difficult: social etiquette in a house of mourning or gestures of religious ceremony at the altar. He learns that what appears formal is involved and fraught: "how complex and mysterious were certain institutions of the Church" (*D* 13). By institution he means the history of the church in its visual rituals and the history of its magisterium in its authority; this authority and institutional history, of course, are what Joyce sought to break from in his art. Yet in the word "institution" the boy only incompletely glimpses what he has been taught: the Institution as the words of Christ at the Last Supper is precisely what is at stake in Flynn's crisis in the story and in Joyce's art *of* the story.

The story has the same hiddenness that Joyce saw in the Greek rite. What appealed to Joyce as strange about the Greek Mass is highlighted in Joyce's letter mentioning the "The Sisters" in conjunction with it: "The altar is not visible but at times the priest opens the gates and shows himself. For the Gospel he comes out of a side gate and comes down into the chapel and reads out of a book. For the elevation he does the same. At the end when he has blessed the people he shuts the gates: a boy comes running down the side of the chapel with a large tray full of little lumps of bread. The priest comes after him and distributes the lumps to scrambling believers. Damn droll!" (*Letters* 2:86–87). What is evidently most striking to Joyce is the concealed quality of the ritual: the occluded altar, the opening and shutting of various gates as the priest shows or hides himself.[23] All this showing and hiding strikes Joyce as humorously odd and even diabolical: "Damn droll!" Joyce must have found in this liturgical strangeness and schism something like a "ripping good joke." What also seems to appeal to Joyce is the inexplicability of what he cannot understand from attending the Mass: the helter-skelter distribution of the "lumps of bread"—a substance he will not call "the sacrament" and that he resolutely sees as bread lumps only—and particularly the concealment of some tantalizing meaning in what cannot fully be seen even in plain view or practice. The accustomed ritual of Rome is, in the Greek Mass, rendered alien and confusing. It must have appeared to Joyce to hide as much as it revealed. In his puzzlement, Joyce is very much like the boy in "The Sisters" who sees but cannot fathom. The dead Flynn eludes the boy's narration as the Greek Orthodox priest hides from the congregation. The window of the front parlor which is to reveal the mystery of the priest's death is much like the doors at the chancel behind which the Greek priest hides himself. The suggestive function of the shop's recovering of umbrellas evokes the shadowy revelation of the priest and Host at the Mass, as well as the obscuring of one word by another. The strangeness of the Eastern Mass which would be spoken in Greek is clearly matched to the trinity of words that "sounded strangely" in the boy's ears.

What causes Flynn's sanity to teeter is a mystery in the story; what caused the breakdown that results in his strange behavior is, as with other information in the story, only incompletely suggested. The boy wishes to "look upon" the deadly work of paralysis, as if to see something static was to understand it. The mystery and the boy's attempt to glimpse it in signs are related to the invocation of the Real Presence, yet like the metaphoric identity of that presence, the story can never, through its narrative, reveal the mystery. The narrative can only suggest something, and that something concerns the Mass and the broken chalice: it points to questions about transubstantiation. It is not the loss of a sacramental vessel—it can be replaced (but should not be sold as that would be simony)—that is the crucial issue, as Eliza seems to intimate. There is something more vexing the chalice: "They say it was all right, that it contained nothing, I mean." This "nothing," a point only indirectly raised and imperfectly understood, is certainly crucial to Flynn: if the chalice had contained consecrated wine, transubstantiated into the real presence of Christ, his spilling it would be a seemingly serious insult to the Savior.[24] Nervous about the duties of the priesthood and "you might say, crossed" like the Savior he is to evoke and distribute, Flynn is vexed into madness by the challenged concept of the Real Presence, and he is left to confess to himself and to laugh softly at the droll way in which God's real substance has slipped though his fingers. If there was "nothing" in the chalice, then orthodoxy is nothing. Indeed, if what is in the chalice is only a representation, a figuration or a sign, then his Mass is schismatic: not the Real Presence of Catholic orthodoxy but the consubstantiated Host of heterodox Protestant and Anglican rites. The strangeness of Flynn may be the estrangement of the schismatic; his odd behavior is only an outward sign of the strangeness of his celebration.

And if Flynn's precarious sanity is unsettled by his failed encounter with something other than the orthodox Real Presence in the mystery of schismatic consubstantiation, there are further and similarly troubled spiritual connections central to the shadows of the story. Old Cotter is a man who also deals with spirits: distilled spirits. Acknowledging Flynn's oddity, he says "there was something queer . . . there was something uncanny about him" (D 9–10). The implications of "queer" are firmly behavioral and material: different and alien in action, with the obvious suggestion of sexual impropriety. The "uncanny," however, may be close to the mystery of the story, suggestive as it is of something more than material. It does not merely suggest the unfamiliar in daily routine but (particularly in Northern and Scottish, hence Gaelic, usage apropos to the story) a pervasive instability. The word also suggests, through its opposite, the "canny" ("supernaturally wise, endowed with occult power" [*NED*]), the esoteric knowledge of Rosicrucians or Gnostics and, most particularly, an association with "supernatural powers . . . not quite safe to trust."[25] Particularly pertinent to the arcane happenstance of the dropped chalice, "uncanny" also meant incautious or careless (a sense now obsolete). In a manner similar to "feints" and "worms"—words which seem to represent one thing but refer to something else—that is, the product and the machinery of whiskey distillation—"uncanny" seems to represent the physical and social but actually refers to something more: the workings of the spirit as ineffable and resistant of meaning.

"The Sisters" certainly raises all sorts of questions about the events of the Eucharist and what happens in the work of the Holy Spirit to the elements on the altar. What is in the chalice that Father Flynn dropped is to him a problem concerning the transubstantiated substance of the wine and what is at stake in its accidental spillage. This problem, which also intersects the issue of meaning hidden behind the story's events and the boy's attempt to explain them, is related to the epiclesis in the Eastern and Anglican rites schismatic to the Catholic orthodoxy: the elements of an unorthodox Eucharist are not transubstantiated but remain schismatic as signs and figures.

It is striking how often the story, suggestive and provisional, relies on outward physical details to point to the meaning in the mystery. The boy only confirms the death of Father Flynn—that is, the efficaciousness of the "deadly work" of paralysis—only when he goes to the shop in front of the death room. The words of Cotter, themselves incomplete, are not enough testimony to confirm the event. At the physical address in Little Britain street, where the boy can do as he wishes, he seeks to know what has happened within. (That address, Little Britain Street, represents a schism by pointing to the figuration of the Protestant, Anglican Mass.) Yet he must first satisfy himself by looking at the outside of the building, attempting to read what is visible on the surface. He reads the death card in the shop window, a clear sign of what has actually occurred, and that card stands in for what on "ordinary days" is the "notice," "Umbrella Recovered." That notice is "not visible now," because the death card has obscured the ordinary, hidden the everyday. The little shades that are covered over (in a manner consistent with the obscuring process in the story that masks words like "Gnostic" behind "gnomon" or "rheumatic" behind "pneumatic") have given way to the great shade, death. "Notice," of course, is related to knowledge, and even to *gnosis*, so the boy's orthodox quest is continually thwarted by the schismatic.

The story represents other attempts at confirming inward causes by the act of looking outward. When Father Flynn had disappeared from the parish house (much as the priest disappears in the strange Greek Mass Joyce observed), the other priests are said to seek him out: they "looked high up and low down," going to the chapel "to look for him" even though physically they "couldn't see a sight of him" (*D* 18). These attempts only confirm the tenuous equivalence of the outward and visible with the inward and spiritual.

This issue of meaning barely accessible by signs, that fundamental schismatic turn of Protestantism, is also a frequent feature of the other stories in the collection. While the first three stories of *Dubliners*, written over three years, contain clear acts of remembrance of an intricate past, as does the unorthodox Eucharist, the three stories written immediately after "The Sisters"—"Eveline," "After the Race," and "Clay"—contain substitutable signs, as does a consubstantiated Mass. From the heavy-handed ending of "Race" (1904), "Daybreak gentlemen!" (*D* 48), illumination seems always to be just beyond the reach of each character. About to embark with Frank, with the black "mass" of the boat looming beyond as she grasps the "rails"—a re-creation of the moment of the distribution of the Eucharist at the supper—Eveline gives "no sign of love or . . . recognition" (*D* 41), so that there is no communion between her and Frank, no outward configuration of what is inward and invisible. The boy in "Araby" (1905) must likewise view the world as sigla: trying to convince his uncle—the authority in his world—to allow him the freedom to go the bazaar located ominously in the East, he eagerly observes him hang up his coat, noting gnomically, "I could interpret these signs" (*D* 33). The end of "Clay" (written in 1905 and first given the more overtly religious title "All Hallow's Eve") has a similar moment of failed memory and unrecognized sign: the repeated song verse and the failure to recognize the clay in the game. Maria is urged to "take a glass of wine" (*D* 105) to become more open and expressive. If her confused singing is caused by this rare communion, its other, major, effect is to make her full of "reminiscences" (*D* 105). Her work with Protestant women may have turned her into a schismatic. Joe is so moved by her song that he cannot "find what he was looking for" (*D* 106), blind to the visible opener of the spirit he wishes to consume. The Real Presence of Joyce's mimetic reality has come down, in the damn drollery of Joyce's misbelief, to spirits in a bottle. The ending of "Ivy Day" has the afflatus of Henchey's poem met by the exploding gasses of the spirits of porter when the spirit of Parnell fails to come to a summons of reluctant believers (another sort of epiclesis).

Often such "misread" signs in the stories are a confusion about inward erotic meanings of the sort that the church would find beneath notice. Joyce's rupture with orthodoxy in the service of narrative allows him license to freely express this sort of meaning (as we shall see in the next chapter). Mr. Duffy, pious in his self-regard, misreads Mrs. Sinico's "every sign of unusual excite-ment" (*D* 111). Gabriel is similarly obtuse when he fails to understand Gretta's physical posture in the Gresham room: "If only she would turn to him. . . . he must see some ardour in her eyes first" (*D* 217). When she runs from him to cry at the remembrance of the song (her private narrative of a personal past), he stands "stockstill for a moment in astonishment" and then looks at himself in the cheval-glass, at his face which "always puzzled him when he saw it" (*D* 218). Many inward meanings can be missed in outward signs.

Thus the small and incorrect word "epicleti" works very large consequences. The first consequence is a rupture with Roman orthodoxy pure and simple; the second consequence is an art that is conceived and modeled as a description. In its challenge to Roman orthodoxy as a schismatic choice, epiclesis insists on a figurative event, not a literal one: thus it is open to representation and mimesis. It is a dramatic representation rather than Real Presence, thus a narrative ac-count rather than an actual process. As a narrative, it evokes something of the past, something to be remembered, that requires memory and recall. It marks a movement of change and development. All these appeal to Joyce because they challenge Rome and thus allow him to marshal the constitutive parts of the art he intends to create. The schismatic turn in epiclesis establishes early for Joyce an art of narrative, the shifting elusiveness of words (the medium of narration) as signs, and the metaphoric substitutability of art and real life. The thematic benefits of schism continue, moreover, long after he has established his claim to rebellion against dogma in his person and his art.

### 3

If epiclesis is the alpha of Joyce's schismatic turn, that word and issue at the very beginning of his art, the omega must be his interest at the latter end in the *Wake* in the Eastern position (again leaning to the heterodox) of the pro-cession of the Holy Ghost. Ever consistent with his own rebelliousness, Joyce knew that the Holy Ghost evoked by the epiclesis had further schismatic ideas he could adapt for art. The mystery of the Trinity is another of the great intel-lectual problems of Christian thought, one that has attracted much attention that leans toward the extreme of the heretical, largely because the Trinity, as a distribution of power and identity, is about authority. From the earliest years of the church, even when it was one body, there were questions regarding the relations among the persons of the Trinity in the notion of filiation: is Jesus divine, human, or both; is he related to the Father; how does the Holy Ghost proceeds from the two, son and father. The issues of Christ's nature and of his relation to the Father are subjects of heresies led by Sabellius and Arius respectively. Stephen, true to his schismatic wishes, is fascinated by these heresiarchs; he is so, in part, because their questions challenge notions of relations between affiliated fathers and sons. The last issue of the Trinity, how the Holy Ghost relates to the other persons of the Trinity, is our concern here. The particular narrow issue of this relationship, like so many of Joyce's interests in heretical positions, is less important for its actual facts than for its wider attractions as a challenge and as art. Not merely an esoteric issue, it is one that tracks notions crucial to Joyce's career: rebellious response to authority and questions of affiliation, both as expressions of autonomy and identity.

The procession of the Holy Ghost, as it is called, furthered the rupture already caused between Rome and Constantinople over the epiclesis; according to the *Catholic Encyclopedia*, "schismatic Greeks maintain that the Holy Ghost, true God like the Father and the Son, proceeds from the former alone" ("Holy Ghost," 7:411). Catholic orthodoxy holds that "The Holy Ghost is God, consubstantial with the Father and the Son. . . . He proceeds, not by way of generation, but by way of spiration." On these connections rests the mystery of the Trinity, and the questions which followed logically from the debates about Christ's substance continued to strain relations between East and West. The procession of the Holy Ghost is for Catholic orthodoxy established in the Nicene Creed with the formula "Ex Pater Filioque procedit." To reject the filioque clause is to be freed not only from Catholic orthodoxy, but to partake of the same liberating sense of rejecting all bonds of various connections of power and the limits they involve.

In some measure, rejection of the bonds of paternal connection, with their implications of subordination to authority, appeals to Stephen. He resists those claims in *Ulysses*, where he is fascinated with questions of relationships, largely because he wishes to resist his own biological connection to his father Simon. He considers in "Proteus" the issues of Trinitarian relations as expressed in the Nicene Creed. Somewhat perversely, the figure of Jesus appeals to Stephen not on any religious grounds, but from the fact that the Son is said to be begotten of the Father, not made by the biology that connects Stephen regrettably to the "man with his eyes"; Stephen is, by contrast, "made not begotten" (*U* 3.45). Thus, he engages in his psychomachia through means of church doctrine, not at all a surprising sublimation: when Stephen thinks about the heresiarchs such as Arius (*U* 3.50), or earlier Photius (1.656) and Sabellius (1.659), he does so because of his own discomfort with relationships. Sabellius challenged the notion that there were three persons in the Trinity, arguing rather that God manifested himself variously as one modal of the three, that God was monophysite—one nature, but three modes. Arius argued that there was a gradation among the three persons, not an equality. Photius, that bishop instrumental in separating Constantinople from Rome, furthered the rupture by this claim of Filiation. These three figures are the ones characterized by the *Catholic Encyclopedia* as those "schismatic Greeks" who maintain that the Holy Ghost proceeds from the God only ("Holy Ghost," 7:409). All heresiarchs challenge orthodoxy, and we shall see (in chapter 5) how Stephen—and Joyce—creatively seek to establish these and other figures not only as resisters to church power but as local political figures of a nationalist bent.

Stephen resists the various connections of the Son with the Father and of the Holy Ghost with either or both, obviously because he seeks his own autonomy. He resists all sorts of filiations that seek to diminish his possibilities for freedom. The schismatic turn is just such a gesture, a challenge to authority of the magisterium, of connections of domination and of obedience. Fascination with such issues, long ago sources of schism, continues late into Joyce's career and is explained in a letter he dictated to Lucia in 1933. In this letter to his onetime close friend Frank Budgen, Joyce reported that the Augustiner Kirche of their shared Zurich had departed from Rome in the year of papal infallibility, which was itself a good example of "Mookse gone Gripes." The phrase had clearly come to be for Joyce an example of rebellion and splitting off over an issue of church dogma. Joyce draws Budgen's attention to the so-named passage in the *Wake* that enacts the "schism between western and eastern christendom" to point out that "all the grotesque words in this are russian or greek for the three principals dogmas that separate Shem from Shaun"—to wit, the Immaculate Conception, the procession of the Holy Ghost, and papal infallibility (*Letters* 3:284). Shem and Shaun are no less than the related siblings of a unit constituted necessarily by complementary opposites, so that filiation and rebellion are enfolded into them: they are, in turn, orthodoxy and heterodoxy, authority and schism. Even Joyce's daughter, herself riven into contested parts but very much the filiated daughter of her father, recognizes the persistence of the schismatic turn to the creation of this passage.

The paragraph noted (156.089–17) represents the confrontation of Mookse and Gripes, particularly the Russian and Greek churches (but also the Irish) with Rome, as the prototype of all schisms, characterized as a series of lamentable oppositions ("sadcontras"), causing breakups and successions ("allbusts . . . seceded"). The operative term is "raskolly," Russian for schism, but containing always possibilities of a ludic freedom that comes from breaking *any* strictures. The three issues highlighted, themselves a trinity of causes of rupture, appear in short order in the paragraph. Because these issues are most recent in church history, they are not causes of long-ago established schisms, but rather reinforce the historical evolution of dogma; they were for Joyce a most evident part of the arbitrary nature of truth: the Immaculate Conception (1854) and papal infallibility (1869, the cause of Augustiner Kirche's dissent). These are represented, respectively, by the Russian "allspillouts" and "nepogreasymost." While the Russian words act as an estranging device of alien language (and alphabet), the English of "allspillouts" (immaculate) certainly indicates a dispersion and loss of containment, an implied incontinence which typifies a rupture from the containing authority of Rome. "Nepogreasymost" makes papal infallibility a most unattractive notion, complete with nepotistic motives and unctuous responses. The power that Infallibility granted the Pope, Joyce well knew, would only lead to servile truckling. Continuing suggestions of looseness and liquidity beyond a central control, Joyce renders the Greek for the procession of the Holy Ghost as "archeporoozers of his haggyown pneumax," adding, with "pneumax" (like "thorax"), a sense of something clinical and unappealing. (The word "haggyown" suggests the haggis, another hodgepodge of sheep's stomach and windpipe.) Because, as we are arguing, Joyce's endings are his beginnings, it is worth remarking that the story "Grace" reflects directly on the notion of papal infallibility, with its greatly inaccurate chronicle of the debate; it also has the exchange where McCoy provides Kernan with the very clinical appraisal of his injuries by nominating the "thorax."[26]

The Russian for procession of the Holy Ghost—"breadchestviousness"— also comes out in the passage as something physical, something connected with the quotidian in life or art. There is, Joyce knew, something not only sustaining in art (whatever sustenance the daily bread of religion might provide), but something devious. Both art and religion are metaphor, even as they are both a trick.

The Russian and Greek terms in the passage themselves make the break from the church and language of Rome. Yet the source of the tension returns in its Latin form at the end of the paragraph. The filioque clause is parodied at the last as a sort of swift dismissal or kick in the head—"got the hoof from his philioquus"—but it, too, has had its origin in something physical and potentially sickening: the "monophysicking" from earlier in the paragraph. The Monophysites taught that there is but one nature of Christ, not one both human and divine. As a result, the Holy Ghost cannot proceed from Christ and the Father, but only the Father. Sabellius was Monophysitism's foremost proponent, although he is merely shadowed in the Wake passage after his appearance in Ulysses. (We will see how Joyce makes this figure into a nationalist as well as a schismatic in chapter 5.)

The passage uses all these terms from the Eastern Church and makes more alien the appeal of the historical Great Schism by including the Russian with the Eastern. ("Raskol" not only means schism in Russian, but, by being in that language, seems to enfold the larger disruption of the Russian Revolution.) However, as always with Joyce, the passage points to his alienation from his native Dublin. "Raskoly," rascally, suggests the ludic possibilities in schismatic rupture Joyce portrayed much earlier in the Whitsuntide entertainment at Belvedere College in *Portrait*, when the rector was "taken off" in a "ripping good joke." (Joyce's fierce logic must be admired: Whitsunday is the Feast of Pentecost, the descent on the apostles of the Holy Ghost.) The "Mookse and Gripes" episode is also about the Church of Ireland in potential break with Rome, a local church threatened by the central authority and resistant to its filiated connections. And there is something else alien but also uncannily familiar in this *Wake* passage: the Greek terms here cast shadows back to the origin of Joyce's turn to schism in the Eastern Church by covering and reflecting, like the umbrella and the candles, the Greek words from that original story "The Sisters." Papal infallibility is an issue that highlights the arbitrary nature of dogma in "Grace," and that story, Gabler notes, has some connection to "The Sisters"; Joyce was consistent in remembering (and using) his schisms.

Looked at in this light, with the sense that this passage might make visible something about the process of artistic schism that was vaguely present but hidden long before, we find two signal words from "The Sisters." "Parysis" (155.16) may be the Paris that is worth a Mass, but it also is similar to that maleficent word in the beginning of the story, "paralysis." Likewise, "russicruxian" (155.28) may be the puzzle of Russia, but it is also the mystery of its Eastern Church and, most tellingly, what the uncle calls the unnamed boy narrator, "that rosicrucian" (*D* 11). A word like "archeporoozers" seems also to signal the origins of Joyce's schismatic turn, as both "arche" and "parousia" suggest onsets and beginnings. The "base semenoyous" (which McHugh glosses as "semionon," Greek for sign) evokes the signs that are so elusive in "Sisters," those products of the emphasis on the metaphoric substitution of the schismatic Greek Mass. Yet the possible reading of "semen" brings up the biology Stephen wishes to avoid by his own rejection of his filiation with Simon his maker/father, natural connections which the boy in "The Sisters" avoids by being raised by aunt and uncle. Biology does not explain the filiation of Father and Son, as the latter is begotten, not made.

There is a hovering presence over this passage from the *Wake*, not unlike the hovering presence said to be one property of the Holy Ghost. "Haggyown pneumax" (for Holy Ghost) may be a shadow cast by the Eastern aura of "The Sisters" in Eliza's "rheumatic wheels" and the church of the heretical Gnostic, the Hagia Pneuma. The greatest hovering presence in the story, like the Holy Ghost, is that of the deceased Father Flynn himself. Several terms in this passage from the *Wake* seem to body forth that figure from the first story, starting with a term that seems to refer to burial: "sarnaktiers," with its suggestion of the flesh (*sarkos*) and something naked (German *nakt*), as well as the tomb (sarcophagus). The story draws repeated attention to Flynn's "heavy grey face" (*D* 11) and to his being "coffined" (*D* 12). In the *Wake* passage, the very physical term "combuccinate" (with the sense of the Mookse trumpeting his ideas, but also perhaps a pun on the Holy Ghost as deriving from "spiration") draws attention to the cheeks and mouth which figure so prominently in the boy's images of Flynn: his large "lips" and protruding "tongue"(*D* 11, 13). More distantly, the notion of the immaculate in "aspillouts" would certainly not immediately call to mind Flynn's dirty and "stained" cassock but for the fact that those stains came from "the constant showers of snuff" "that dribbled though his fingers" (*D* 12), images again of lack of control and incontinence that run through the *Wake* passage and signify the rupturing looseness made by schism.

One last and slight shadow of absence in "The Sisters" seems to appear later in the last things of the *Wake*: the empty chalice in the story is one of the mysteries that causes Flynn great distress and the boy much puzzlement about the nature of the Real Presence at the Mass. There is no wine in the paragraph under examination (although obviously the Gripes is a shrunken cluster of grapes in the story). One other way to see something at work in the Russian term for procession, glossed as "breadchestviousness," is to find what is missing from the elements in the failed semblance of a Mass of no presence in the "The Sisters": the pyx or bread box ("chest") which holds the wafer, the complement to the empty chalice Flynn takes to the grave. An element of deviousness surrounds the pyx as it does the chalice, an uncertainty that calls forth (like an epiclesis) a need for the metaphoric substitution represented by the art of schism.

With metaphor and the Protestant position on the Eucharist, Joyce comes to rip again the fabric of his Catholicism. The epiclesis as one cause of the Great Schism might be said to be the origin of all schisms; it is also the origin of Joyce's artistic misbelief. Yet the schism with the East had, as is always in the case of historical events, other causes as well. One other source of contention between Rome and Constantinople was the issue of the distribution of episcopal power, and thus of hegemony, which continually fascinated Joyce. The product of the second great schism of the Reformation, in particular the Anglican Church, has a liturgy with further heretical consequences of a political, artistic, and even nationalist nature. Joyce's own persistent interest in schismatic Anglican worship will be the subject of the next chapter.

# 4

# The Literary Advantages of Protestantism

Let us return briefly to the text in *Portrait*, which raised the notion of schism to find in it another matter of rending, the verse that Heron tells Stephen to parody, the definition of a heretic in Matthew's Gospel: "let him be to theea as the heathena and the publicana" (*P* 76). We remarked in passing that Heron seems to recite the line inaccurately with reference to both the Catholic Bible's Douay version ("let him be to thee as the heathen and publican") and the Authorized English Bible, the King James Version ("let him be unto thee as an heathen man and a publican"). Here we will discuss the consequences of that inaccuracy. In another allusive appeal to scripture and a similar conflation of sources, Stephen characterizes the dean of studies, before joining the discipleship of the Catholic Church, as having "sat at the receipt of custom" (*P* 189), a phrasing identical in all three synoptic Gospels in both Douay and the Authorized Version. There are two issues here: the first and lesser one is which Bible in English is alluded to, as this issue has consequences for Joyce's freedom of choice; the second and greater, is the fact that the Bible is used as a source of authority and substantiation.

To appeal to the Bible at all is a striking move for a Catholic, indoctrinated in obedience to the clergy in its intercessory power to inform and lead. To seek and to derive authority by reading and citing directly from scripture rather than receiving it from ecclesiastical authorities (ranked from the priest up to the Pope) is a striking move of independent agency and individual choice. The Butler Catechism makes very clear that reading the Bible is a derivative, mediated process; "clergy are required to read" the scriptures, "but there is no such general obligation incumbent on the laity; it being sufficient that they listen to it from their pastors." According to the Deharbe Catechism, the faithful are enjoined "to listen and hear" the scriptures, not to read them. By contrast to Catholic indirections, Thomas Cranmer demands of the Protestant faithful that they "read, mark, learn, and inwardly digest"; the process is one of privately and directly assimilating scripture.[1] Stanislaus notes (of his own instruction at Belvedere, but pertinent as well to his brother's) "that in Catholic homes and in Catholic schools the Bible is never read. In all the years I was at . . . Belvedere, never once was the English Bible, or Douay version, or Latin Vulgate opened or read or discussed in and out of class."[2] To read the Bible on one's own, following the pattern of the lectionary or the inclination of individual interest, was the manner of the schismatics of the Western Schism and the Reformation. In fact, Stanislaus asserts that, never opening a Bible but following his pastor, he "had always been led to regard it as a Protestant book."[3] It was Luther who, in the break with Rome, proposed that scripture alone was the guiding source of authority and conscience, *sola scriptura*. (When, at the 1519 Leipzig Disputation of the ninety-nine theses of Wittenberg, Luther demurred about the fallibility of the court episcopally authorized to challenge him for his own authority, his accuser, Johann Eck, a theological scholar appointed by the bishop, closed the proceeding with a laconic remark: "If you believe a legitimately assembled council can err and has erred, then you are to me as a heathen and publican." This retort was widely circulated in Catholic histories and may well have been known to Joyce.) An expression of protest, the vernacular Bible, accessible to all readers, was in fact an empowering device that wrested from clergy the power of control and the mystery of the Latin. The 1610 Douay English Bible was in fact a late reaction to the various vernacular Bibles, such as Luther's own or the Geneva Bible.

The freedom of agency suggested in this biblical reference would certainly appeal to Joyce; not the piety that comes from tract reading but the rebellious possibility that he could use to defy and outflank the authority of the church by direct appeal to scripture, even if merely by gloss or allusion. In fact, such an autonomy of text seems rigidly consistent with the autonomous authority Joyce accorded to his own written word.[4] What could be more congenial to Joyce than to believe that text and reader together form an authority greater than any outside power? That is a radical position, not only a political one to counter the hegemony of culture and state, but a religious one to challenge the unitary power of Rome.

If the challenge to ecclesiastical authority was the major appeal to Joyce of biblical allusion in his texts, there were other purposes as well. Joyce's reference to a specific version of the Bible was rebellious as well. In that most of his citations come from the Authorized Version, that is, the Bible of Britain, Joyce consciously makes another sort of disruptive break of individual choice. He turns to the source of British imperial culture and its power, and in this he turns his back on the growing secular authority of Irish nationalism, which sought to banish traces of Anglo-Saxon culture from an Ireland that was seen increasingly as Gaelic and Catholic. Thus this schismatic impulse of biblical allusion obtains not only as regards breaking from the strictures of Rome but in a turning away of those of nationalism; Joyce proved uncongenial to all persuasions.

Joyce cites the English Bible in his very first essays and throughout his longer works; this citation is of a piece with his active interest in the epiclesis and the resultant representative Eucharist conceived for *Dubliners* that provided him with narrative and figure. Joyce also appeals directly to the Anglican prayer book as another source of schismatic self-authorizing to challenge Rome and Tara. Even as late as *Finnegans Wake* he continues the flirtation when he frequently cites not only the English Bible but also the Anglican Book of Common Prayer.

Let us start with Joyce somewhat early in his career; such apostasy arises at the very beginning of his writing. If, as Stanislaus notes, the Bible was unfamiliar to Catholics, Joyce nevertheless shows a close familiarity with it. The simplest explanation, worthy of Occam, would be to say that the English Bible was so widely published and distributed in the United Kingdom and Ireland that it would be most readily available even to a penurious student such as Joyce.[5] To leave the issue there, however, would be to beg some important questions: first, why Joyce would choose to cite the Bible at all; and second, why he would need to cite the Bible with such detail as to refer to it accurately.

The response to the first question, going beyond Occam, is that to pick up any Bible was to act according to his own needs for reading (religion as *relegere*, a rereading and interpretation). Joyce did so in defiance of the obedience he owed to his college instructors and in the aim of obtaining for himself some certainty and direction to replace those of the magisterium. (In actual practice, a pious Catholic's exposure to the Bible, through portions selected for the daily missals, would be restricted and proscribed by authority.)

The response to the second question would be to remark that Joyce wished to cite in particular the Anglican Bible as a way to countermand the growing Irish insularity about culture and tradition. By allusions and echoes he supports the voice and particular aesthetics he develops in his early essays; one way to claim authority for his arguments is to appropriate scripture. To his already-sure self-confidence—and counterstance—in these first writings, Joyce adds the weight of an authority his own church would not allow him to recognize and his own culture would deny.

Chronologically, the first essay to note is "Royal Hibernian Academy 'Ecce Homo'" (1900). Surely a school assignment, Joyce's choice seems particularly calculated to be a topic approved by his masters that he could in turn subvert by his citation of biblical verses. In describing a weeping figure, probably the Holy Mother, Joyce says, "she is the new figure of lamentation . . . of those . . . who weep and mourn but yet are comforted" (*CW* 34; the last clause insignificantly variable in the Douay and Authorized Version, Jeremiah and Matthew). The use of this phrase ("weep and mourn") for the description of a new Rachel shows Joyce's sensitivity to the power of allusion within the Bible, where the Gospel is intended to echo one of the earlier Hebrew texts, Lamentations. Allusion is a power he seeks to appropriate for his own voice in a school assignment. A description of the raiment worn by the suffering title figure, "red as them that tread in the winepress" (*CW* 37) likewise echoes the Prophet Isaiah and lets Joyce speak with a voice backed up now twice by vatic power (Isaiah and Jeremiah). "Treadeth the wine press" also appears in slightly different form in Revelation, a text to which we will shortly turn in more detail. In a piece of juvenalia and on a religious topic, Joyce demonstrates not merely the ability to cite a passage from scripture but to do so with his own enfranchised authority.

Religious topics were not only the obvious context for biblical references; so too were topics on art, and perhaps that context was most crucial in establishing his agency in contrast to received authority. The essay "Drama and Life," so important to Joyce as his means of asserting himself against the strictures of school and church, was conceived as a polemical piece to be delivered confrontationally at the Literary and Historical Society; it has a clear echo of the Bible from Revelation. It must be noted that the paper is itself a call for something new, something to replace and supercede the art that has come before. So, both in tone and as a proclamation of a new age, it resembles the work of St. John. Joyce asserts that there is a spirit in the lives of men and women in "deeper intimacy" "for whose truth they became seekers" (*CW* 41). This spirit, he says, "is as the roaming air" and never leaves their vision "till the firmament is as a scroll rolled away." This last line alludes unequivocally to Revelation in the King James Version (6:13), as well as to the parallel text from Isaiah (34:3–5). (The Douay shows the lines both places—far less famously if more accurate to the Greek—as "folded like a book.")

The power of Ibsen and that of divine revelation are both served by the prophetic power of rebellious choice, exercised both in the argument of the paper itself and through its schismatic allusion to the biblical text. Joyce achieves that much merely with his choice. So the confrontational aspect of the paper "Drama and Life" is paralleled by the confrontational aspect of biblical citation and, especially, the use of Revelation in the Authorized Version. To choose to cite from scripture enfranchises Joyce as his own authority, and the additional use of the Prophets adds a depth of conviction to these schoolboy essays. It is no coincidence that the subjects of these two essays are art forms—pictorial and dramatic—and that art is to be associated with the heretical choice of a breaking from convention that is equal to (and through allusion, served by) schism in religion.

Such a power of individually achieved authority derived from choice continues through several other early essays, most notably Joyce's first publication "Ibsen's New Drama" (1902). While admittedly written for a larger and more secular audience, one not constrained by Catholic teaching as were his clerics and fellow students, the essay nonetheless continues with biblical allusions. In it, he describes Ibsen's reputation as lagging and states that many years "must pass before he will enter his kingdom" (*CW* 63). This phrase, as frequent in scripture as to be considered common, is one whose appeal to the audience lies in Joyce's claiming that Ibsen is in fact a new Messiah to the arts. Yet there is another phrase in the essay which comes only from the King James Version of the Bible. Praising Ibsen's ability with character, Joyce claims of one created figure: "the hand which has drawn him has not yet lost her cunning"(*CW* 64). This claim echoes Psalm 137:5, "let my right hand lose her cunning"; in the Douay's Psalm 136, the phrase is translated less poetically as "let my right hand be forgotten." Again, this is a phrase well enough known to come into common usage without close biblical reading, but it is unequivocally from the English Bible. Joyce was also fond enough of it to use it again ten years later, this time by way of negation, with reference to another author, Charles Dickens. Dickens' writing about places far from London, Joyce felt, made his magic fail him, "his hand seems to have lost her ancient cunning" ("The Centenary" [1912]; *OCPW* 184). To use a phrase from English culture, if not directly from the English Bible, about Dickens was consistent; to use it about Ibsen was suggestive: as Ibsen challenged the conventional forms of drama, so Joyce breaks with the pieties of his religion and his nationalism.

One more author glossed by allusion to the Protestant Bible was an unlikely one, James Clarence Mangan. Joyce argues his sullen temper and tone are caused by his sufferings which "have cast him inwards, where for many ages the sad and wise have elected to be" (*CW* 76–77). Yet rather than relate Mangan's bleakness to his Irish temperament, a conventional attribution, Joyce draws a biblical parallel: "Naomi would change her name to Mara, because it has gone bitterly with her" (*CW* 80). The exile and alienation of Mangan is well captured by the aptness of Joyce's parallel to Naomi's story, and the same alien quality is further continued by Joyce's exclusive allusion to the Authorized Version. The Douay text of Ruth explains how Naomi changes her name, but only the Authorized Version has the line "The Lord hath dealt bitterly with me." The exile of Naomi and the alienation of Mangan make a forceful similarity. In being aware of this phrase, Joyce uses the schismatic Bible as an alienation from his background: there were advantages to the estrangement of choosing an unorthodox text.

The university lectures at Trieste on English literature also retain these traces. He makes Defoe's Crusoe the quintessential Englishman, with all the tedious virtues of Empire, but Joyce concludes his essay with a strange parallel that continues to connect literature and Protestantism: "The Evangelist saw on the island of Patmos the apocalyptic collapse of the universe and the raising up of the walls of the eternal city . . . Crusoe saw but one marvel in all the fertile creation that surrounded him, a naked footprint in the virgin sand: and who knows if the latter does not matter more than the former?" (*OCPW* 174–75). Human society and the realism of British empiricism seem to weigh as much as revelation, and Joyce, we shall see, was familiar with John's vision.

The subject of these essays are all authors—one Norwegian, two British (and quintessentially so), and one Irish—and to them Joyce grants an elevated status by citing from scripture in his support of them. The dates of the essays (from 1900, 1902, and the Dickens and Defoe in 1912) show a continued application of the Protestant Bible as an added means of Joyce asserting himself in intellectual matters by writing the allusions. As he begins to articulate his judgment of art, he appropriates the authority of a text to aid him in his rebellion from convention.

The familiarity Joyce shows with the English Bible in his years just after Belvedere and University College Dublin is striking, given the lack of its presence in Catholic classrooms and Stanislaus' claim that there was no Catholic Bible in the Joyce household. Moreover, Joyce was not passingly familiar with the Authorized Version (as might be suggested by the cultural frequency of some of the biblical phrases passed into common speech, such as a "right hand" which would "loose its cunning"); he was intimately familiar with it. Joyce's intimacy was such that he not only read it closely but also transcribed it directly—and such transcription was, for a Catholic boy, a very clear marking out of a space of difference.

As a sixteen-year-old college student, Joyce made a transcription of the Apocalypse of Saint John; Scholes notes in the Cornell collection that the manuscript "was copied from the King James Version of the New Testament."[6] This was a highly unusual and intimate rebellious act, given the Catholic practice of not encountering scripture directly. Joyce undertook this odd and uncharacteristic exercise sometime in 1899, on the eve of the century's end; perhaps it was during the summer (when, Costello notes, "it was not college work Joyce was doing").[7] By autumn he had begun working on his paper "Literature and Life" and did so until January of 1900. While that paper on drama marks the important beginning of Joyce's independent thinking, Revelation is the end of ends. "Drama and Life" opens up a career for Joyce; the transcription of the Apocalypse has been hidden and veiled, a sign of its transgressive and schismatic nature.

The circumstances under which he did this copying are unknown. The manuscript is described by Scholes as an autograph manuscript some seventy-four pages "on the versos of fols. 143–69."[8] The last pages are missing: the manuscript ends (at the bottom of a page) with chapter 17, verse 3; the next page extant contains chapter 19, picking up at a corruption of verses 11 and 12, and ends with verse 17. Revelation contains twenty-two chapters in all. Paper was at such a premium in the Joyce household that between 1903 and 1905 Stanislaus used (and numbered) those same pages to write his journal "My Crucible." Why Joyce took so many pages of precious paper to copy out a work which he might have found in other sources is only one of a series of nagging questions, such as why the Joyce household, so bare of all possessions by 1899, might have had a copy of the Authorized Version at all.

The physical properties of the manuscript are themselves odd, certainly given what Joyce's holographs were to become. The manuscript shows a deliberateness and care that suggest a presentation copy: Joyce neatly titles it, in tidy, fair-hand flourishes, the Apocalypse of Saint John, which is the title given to it in the Douay Bible, while in Authorized Version the title appears as the Revelation of St. John the Divine. (The Douay is more faithful to the Greek.) Even at the head of his copy—and the start of his career—Joyce's conflation of orthodox and heterodox is present. Within the manuscript, Joyce's handwriting is more precise and clear than it was to become. He marks chapter and verse (chapter in roman numerals, verses in arabic). He makes interlinear corrections (as in chapter 2, verse 11) and additions (chapter 2, verse 2). Interestingly, he occasionally crosses his letter "s" with a line (chapter 4, verse 10; chapter 5, verse 1). This stricken "s" is sometimes initial, sometimes final, sometimes medial; there seems to be no clear method; even capitalized "S"s show this line (chapter 17, verse 5), and the occurrence increases in frequency as the manuscript goes on. Perhaps the marked "s" is merely a schoolboy flourish or an embellishment of his text to make it resemble an ornamental page from the Book of Kells.

Joyce's use of the Bible has not gone unremarked in earlier criticism, although questions as to his purpose in using it have been overlooked. In her *Joyce and the Bible*, Virginia Moseley takes as a given that Joyce would allude to the Bible without considering that act weighted with the sort of schismatic consequence we are suggesting.[9] She does substantiate, unwittingly, Joyce's conflation of versions of the Bible, noting first off that of all the uses she uncovers, Joyce cites the Vulgate only three times in *Ulysses*, where it is Stephen who, self-conscious of his training, cites them all. She omits the actual misquotation of the parable of the good steward from the Douay Luke in "Grace," although in most cases, she correctly notes, "the meaning of both the Douay and the King James versions seems to apply."[10] Yet there was an immediate use to which Joyce puts this copying like Farrington in "Counterparts." We have seen it in the allusive traces of Revelation in works Joyce wrote for University College in the year immediately after the summer of transcription; in so doing, he slyly confronts his teachers and his audience with the independent audacity that the choice of this text required. The effect persists long after university days, as late as the essay on Dickens in 1912.

Joyce's writing out of the Revelation has further effects; these unfold in time in the later, major fiction. Moseley finds and details, with admirable thoroughness, twenty-two allusions or references to it in *Ulysses*, with most appearing, somewhat appropriately, in "Circe," and nearly all the rest from chapters 12 and 13. She finds two in *Portrait*.[11] In all cases, she notes that the source of meaning might be either the Douay or the King James versions, or both (due in no small part to the relatively straightforward Greek text less likely to complicate translation). Yet the fact that the school years' exercise in mere transcription finds its way into Joyce's major works as well as his minor essays is surely a measure of its importance to Joyce's schismatic purposes and possibilities. Joyce writes out a text to establish his own independence and authority and then, rebellious to his religious upbringing, cites himself.

One later appearance in "Circe" plays with the notions of apostasy and rebellion that characterize Joyce's earliest encounter with the text. The Black Mass envisioned after the exit from Bella Cohen's brothel is a scene naturally filled with the ready (and clichéd) unorthodoxy of counterreligions. Along with the clear parallels to the opening of the novel with Buck's imagined Mass, the scene clearly repeats a line from Revelation in this exchange: "The Voice of the Damned: Htengier Tnetopinmo Dog Drol eht rof, Aiulella!" with a response from "The Voice of All the Blessed, Alleluia, for the Lord God Omnipotent reigneth!" (15.4706–712). For Joyce, who has copied out the text of Revelation (19:6), this mirror reversal plays the double-edged game of citing and erasing, a sort of playfulness that is a good joke in the rebellious establishment of his own authority. (Also the echo of droll in the "drol" might put one in mind of Joyce's claim that the appearance and disappearance of the priest during the schismatic Greek Mass is comically "droll.") Moreover, the interchange of the damned and blessed texts, one reversing the direction of the other, represents visually the dynamic of belief and apostasy; the inverted pattern is like a conversion, a turning away. What Joyce did and believed in 1898 he would still hold in 1922.

The allusions in *Portrait* are pertinent, because that text is a fictional account of those years of youth when Joyce was actually writing down his verbatim copy of Apocalypse. The echoes of Revelation, important to the novel, are used in a crucial point in the development: Father Arnall's talks at the retreat in chapter 2. The parallel is implied: what affects Stephen by hearing is similar to what affected Joyce by copying. The purpose of these sermons is to make the boys consider their human acts in light of divine judgment, to reflect upon the choices they make. Arnall speaks by alluding to Revelation at length:

> The stars of heaven were falling upon the earth like the figs cast by the figtree which the wind has shaken. The sun, the great luminary of the universe, had become as sackcloth of hair. The moon was bloodred. The firmament was as a scroll rolled away. The archangel Michael, the prince of the heavenly host, appeared glorious and terrible against the sky. With one foot on the sea and one foot on the land he blew from the archangelical trumpet the brazen death of time. The three blasts of the angel filled all the universe. Time is, time was but time shall be no more. At the last blast the souls of universal humanity throng towards the valley of Jehoshaphat . . . (*P* 113)

Compare 6:12–13 in the Authorized Version—"the sun became as sackcloth of hair" / "and the stars of heaven fell unto the earth as a fig tree casteth her untimely figs," and in the Douay, "the sun became as sackcloth of ashes" / "and the stars from heaven fell upon the earth as the fig tree casteth its green figs." Revelation: "time no longer." Apocalypse: "time shall be no longer."

These parallels evidently function in thematic ways related to fear and excessive punishment, as Joyce grounds them in Stephen's temporary conversion to piety. The plot suggests that Stephen reneges on his choice because of that fear and thus seeks to change and amend his life. The character does not persist in his sinful behavior that was, as a choice, a sort of heresy.

The fear the Last Things stir in the youthful Stephen is inversely related to Joyce's conscious (and cool) transcription of Revelation during his youth, and this proportion of fictional fear to actual choice replays the exchange of timorous orthodox submission (if only temporary in the text) and independent rebellious apostasy that marks Joyce's life.

The ends to which Joyce puts his labor of transcription are, however, limited; in the passages Joyce cites, there is practically no difference between the Authorized Version and the Douay. What differences are there are merely slight choices of translation—prepositions ("unto earth/upon earth"; "fight with/fight against")—or differences in translating nouns more particular in the Greek: "green fig/unripe fig" are two correct versions of the Greek word for a fig that (according to Liddell and Scott) does not ripen but remains green. When the uses to which Joyce put Revelation are examined, there seems to be no reason for his transcribing the Authorized Version, when the Douay, which would certainly have been available at the college, would have been just as accurate. So what remains must be the opportunity Joyce's choice afforded for those sorts of openings and ruptures that lead to error and possibly to freedom.

Joyce shows through these references in *Portrait's* chapter 3 that even priests can err and fall into quotation from the forbidden other. Arnall, in his rather set piece about the Last Things, uses one line that comes only from the King James Version: "the firmament was as a scroll rolled away" (a phrase we saw Joyce use in the essay "Drama and Life"; for him, the stakes of art were apocalyptic). So Joyce's efforts at transcription did produce results of an unambiguous kind that slyly give a Protestant gloss to a Jesuit Father and his effect on Stephen.

There is even a further, if more elaborate, sectarian dig at Arnall and his sermon. The retreat opens with his citing a line inexact on two counts: "'Remember only thy last things and thou shalt not sin forever,' words taken . . . from the Book of Ecclesiastes, seventh chapter, fortieth verse" (*P* 108). Pointing out that the Douay shows the sentence as "In all thy works remember the last things," Thrane rightly notes that Joyce wanted "to satirize his preacher's learning," as the text is not in Ecclesiastes (whose seventh chapter has only thirty verses) but in Ecclesiasticus. Thrane claims that "both the translation and the blunder were probably deliberate on Joyce's part" (277n10). To misquote doctrinally accepted Catholic sources plays right into Joyce's schismatic tendencies, of course; and, in order to make this satire, Joyce would have had to consult the original texts of both books of scripture to establish the errors. Another likely source for the line Arnall quotes is not, as Thrane suggests, the Pinamonti "Hell Opened to Christians" but the Butler Catechism: "Q. What are the four last things to be remembered? A. 1. Death 2. Judgment 3. Heaven 4. Hell." The Catechism was acceptable reading, and priests would have expected their faithful to know it well and firsthand.

One reason why Joyce would have spent his ink and paper, as well as his energies on transcription is that the copying and the reading must have been particularly ink-stained and wholly literal acts of apostasy and rebellion. Close scrutiny and citation of the Word for the sake of gaining authority are rebellious acts. The transcribing of the particular section of the New Testament, innocuous as it might appear, must have been in itself a gesture of *non serviam* direct at the highest authorities in Joyce's life. Millennial issues were of no standing in the Catholic Church. The *Catholic Encyclopedia* notes that millennial concerns do not "appear as a universal doctrine of the Church or as part of the Apostolic tradition" ("Millennium and Millenarianism," 10:308). Augustine held that there would be no Second Coming, although Joachim de Flores did;

Flores is mentioned by Stephen in "Proteus" (3.108), along with other heretics of the church we noted earlier. Millenarianism was of so little consequence in Catholic theology that it is accorded no position, heretical or otherwise. Yet concern for the Second Coming was essentially Protestant and, as such, became for Joyce yet another gesture of apostasy beyond his simply citing the Protestant Bible. Protestantism of the sixteenth century, according to the *Catholic Encyclopedia*, "ushered in the new epoch of millenarian doctrines." To show any sort of interest in the Second Coming, as so mystically acknowledged in the Revelation, was heterodoxy for a student enrolled in a Catholic university. The schismatic impulse of the direct reading of scripture, along with the claim of epiclesis in the stories, are both features of Reformation theology, and both seem to be consistent with the interest in millennialism. Joyce could be quite a logical schismatic. The Revelation was subversive; it marked him in secret as different: perhaps that is why Joyce chose to write it out.

Certainly, the mythic (and nearly enigmatic) symbolism of numerology, types, and figures in the vision of St. John would have appealed to Joyce. Revelation is a text at one and the same time literal and symbolic, a powerful combination that Joyce would increasingly adopt in his works.[12] And such arcana stayed with him a long time: in Joyce's beginning is also his end. St. John, appearing in his own text, asks an angel for the "little book," which he is to eat: he "ate it up: and it was in my mouth as sweet as honey: and as soon as I had eaten it, my belly was bitter" (10:10). Forty years later (a biblical time frame), Shem the Penman—himself his own book—will use the end product of his digestion to make "synthetic ink," and he writes on "romeruled stationery" so "that an Anglican ordinal . . . may ever behold the brand of scarlet on the brow of her of Babylon" (185.10). All the elements are here: the copy book pages (ruled), the excretion of the digested scroll, the tension between Rome and Canterbury, and the reference to the figure in Revelation of the scarlet whore of Babylon. A text only transcribed by Joyce would last him a long time and serve many of his independent ends. As the figure of Shem is one version of Joyce, the schismatic impulse leads not only to art but to self-identification.

Perhaps the private transcription of secret apostasy and cultural cross-dressing occurs because Joyce was flirting with Protestantism while at the same time being wary of its claims to control. True always to his impulse to break away from authority, this interest in the Millennium would challenge not only Catholicism, but the established Anglican religion, and even Irish literary culture. There are two precedents for this challenge close to Joyce's hand. With reference to the Church of Ireland, the foremost millenarian proponent of the mid-nineteenth century was one John Nelson Darby, a Trinity College graduate, who successfully read for the bar and became a clergyman in Wicklow.

His interpretations of Revelation attracted millenarian followers to three meet-
ings at Powerscourt (1831, 1832, 1833), and he greatly influenced the Plymouth
Brothers in England. In Darby's millenarianism, then, Joyce would have found
a challenge in nearby Wicklow to Anglicanism and Catholicism both. It is possible that Darby is remembered later in Joyce's work and included in at least one
of the three uses of the name in the *Wake*: "ere Molochy wars bring the devils
era, a slip of time between a date and a ghostmark, rived by darby's chilldays
embers" (473.09). Michael's wars in heaven on behalf of orthodoxy, conflated
also with Moloch and the devil's own heterodoxy, suggest a time between day
and night ("date" and "ghostmark") and also a point when "time is no more,"
when, as John predicts, the sun shall be extinguished ("chilldays embers") at
the end of the world in Darby's millennium. Much of what Joyce wrote out in
1899 remained with him, providing opportunity that always accompanied his
schismatic gestures.

Thus the flirtation with the millennialism established by Revelation would
pile schism upon schism: a thumb in the eye to the oppressive authority of the
Roman Church, yet also a challenge to the Anglican from one who was not
even a believer. To be true to his nature, so inveterately inclined to rupture,
Joyce would challenge Rome by way of Canterbury, and then turn to challenge
the latter.

Yet there was another Irish orthodoxy Joyce would challenge by transcribing
the Apocalypse—that of the Irish literary establishment. To copy out the Revelation tediously and exactly would be to counter the vague and varied ideas of
the Theosophists as Yeats promulgated them. Rather than refer to the farrago
of cycles and visions and penumbras cribbed from many sources, some actual
and some imagined, Joyce would go to an established text of clear provenance
by way of making a contrast.[13] To challenge the Church of Rome he would write
out a text in order to have it unmediated by their authority; to rebel against the
church of high art in Dublin he would cite a text they would find authoritative
and unwelcome. In both cases he would stand apart from pieties declared in
his own apostasy.

It was also culturally and politically subversive to refer to Revelation in un-
expected ways within the spaces Joyce occupied in 1898. It was a stance counter
to the fellowship of the college in ways that were not just religious. To copy the
King James Version of the Bible was to embrace, while in the arms of an alma
mater that was Catholic, the great text of the Anglican Church. Yet the Authorized Version was more than that. It was also the great book of traditional
English literature and culture. Scholes and Kain claim that Joyce copied out
King James to "demonstrate his familiarity with the 'Protestant' Bible."[14] Surely
this is a tedious and, for Joyce, an uncharacteristically understated way to make

such a demonstration, given, as we have noted, the slight variations between the Douay and the King James versions. The translated Greek text offers neither as many problematic words as the Hebrew of the Old Testament, nor does it use the metaphoric and unusual Greek of the Gospels. Nor, for that matter, is the language of Revelation as resonant with Jacobean rhythms and diction (of which Stephen is inordinately fond in chapter 5 of *Portrait*) as are, say, the Psalms. (We will consider Joyce's preference and familiarity with the Protestant version of the Psalms as late as the *Wake*.) The exegetical differences were of less account for Joyce than were the cultural ones. At the time when the students at University College Dublin were concerned with Irish culture by asserting a claim against Yeats' *Countess Cathleen* and against the "English manners" the Irish theater seemed to import, Joyce was openly against their provinciality; in secret, in his own places and on his own paper, he was making league with the enemy, unCatholic, unIrish. The Irish Literary Theatre's produced *Countess Cathleen* in May of 1899; we must surmise that Joyce's transcription of Revelation occurred that same summer. To separate himself from the multitude took courage in allied contexts; while he refers to Bruno's martyrdom, he has other heresies in mind: not to be an observant Catholic but to assert individual authority, not to be a slavish nationalist but to embrace a larger, if hegemonic, culture. The transcription of Revelation seemed to well serve these ends.

To be consistent in his aims and logical in his thought, Joyce would find it necessary to refrain from assenting to any unitary identity, because to do so would be to compromise his freedom and limit his expression. When such an identity was the Catholic Church, he would resist its authority by engaging in acts of misbelief, by striking out in directions that led away from the unity of the magisterium to the ruptures of schisms like those of the Eastern Church and the Reformation. When family duty called him to attend his mother's deathbed or to support his sisters, he chose instead to decline and to make his own family. When the unified thinking was the call of the nation, Joyce turned from its siren call to flee to the Continent; there, he could form his person in exile and his literature in association with foreign literary models.

And when nationalism combined with Catholicism to produce a definition of Irish identity that was as rigidly monolithic as possible, Joyce had no choice but to resist. He valued freedom and autonomy, asserting that "the economic and cultural conditions of the homeland do not permit the development of individuality" (*CW* 171). Religion was political, Joyce understood, nearly everywhere but most particularly in his own country. Joyce was unequivocal in believing that getting rid of Britain would not matter if Ireland were to remain under the sway of Rome. As late as the essay "Saints and Sages," he makes clear a claim he believed from his university days: "I confess [a most telling word in the context of religion and politics] that I do not see what good it does to fulmi-nate against English tyranny while the tyranny of Rome still holds the dwelling place of the soul" (CW 173). It is no accident that the battleground is the soul, which animates the self and its freedom. Joyce recognized that the powers of church and Tara were political and equal. "Ireland has so far been the Catholic Church's most faithful daughter," he notes, too loyal and also too chaste (CW 169). Joyce was prescient in this belief. "Most Catholics" of the time, one critic notes, "would have regarded [that claim of religion as political] as applying only to Protestantism," but when "the main feature distinguishing the Irish from the English was their Catholicism," "it remained a powerful source of nationalism."[15]

This powerful combination required Joyce's resistance. He would stand against nationalist piety that was equal to that of the church; he would resist the church's claim to an allegiance both in this world and the next. He would reject the nationalist claims for purity even as he would refuse to accept the church's idealization of actual life. And this resistance, breaking from church and nation, took a turn that would enable him to be contrarian and heterodox to the very core.

If Joyce's apostatic schism against Catholic dogma in his use of the Prot-estant Bible (and Reformation allusions to it) took place early, then equally early was his breaking with nationalist ideological orthodoxy; in fact, the two contrary breaks occur at the same time and with the same motive. Joyce was consistent in his heretical choices, claiming to value logic above all else. If he were to reject Catholicism's unitary and monolithic claims to truth, he would also reject those nationalist claims to authenticity, especially as the latter were based so heavily on the former. What he would save of his own by breaking with the church hierarchy he would not so easily give over to Irish nationalist mediocrity.

Mediocrity was what he called it. Joyce's first year of university in 1899 (the year he began his transcription of the Apocalypse) saw another of his writings (and another sort of revelation): "The Day of the Rabblement." This essay was Joyce's response to the students' provincial protest at the Irish Theatre produc-tion of the Countess Cathleen in May of that year. (It would be too much to sug-gest that the events around the production were extreme enough to make Joyce turn to the apocalyptic text.) Censored by college authorities on the grounds of immorality (a fiat that confirmed Joyce's fears about being silenced), "Rabble-ment" was privately published only later in 1901. It is clear that the essay sets out Joyce's disdain for common nationalist sentiment and vocabulary precisely because of their connection with the church. The students' response and Joyce's challenge mirror the issue exactly.

In the "Letter of Protest" published in the *Freeman's Journal*, the students claim that the play "offers as a type of our people a loathsome brood of apostates."[16] As much as Joyce certainly would have welcomed the exclusionary and liberating charge of apostasy in his private schism, he would have recoiled at the unitary and racial assumption of the phrase "our people." The Irish were no more a monolith than the church was one; Joyce always asserted the possibilities of the individual, whether situated in a church or a neighborhood. Only in a gesture of rupture and a concomitant assertion of possibility could Joyce free himself from the claims of nationhood and church that were psychological and physical: he names them "fetishism" and "contagion" and claims that they deluded the mind into "self-deception" (*CW* 71).

To read a student editorial in response to Joyce's essay in the college magazine *St. Stephen's* is to be completely convinced of the rightness of Joyce's attitude toward his fellow students' unthinking acceptance of Catholic teaching and easy assumption of Irish racial virtues.[17] The editorial articulates explicitly the tacitly accepted values that surrounded Joyce and that he sought to resist by the contrarian attitude that was forming for him in the schismatic gesture. Defending the students, the editor claims that they "clung to a standard of morality—the tradition of the Catholic Church, the ethical teaching of Christendom."[18] A dogmatic morality that must be "clung to" was indeed a straw to grasp at, as the world seemed to this rabble to be slipping from the high perch of morality into an implied morass of licentious sexuality and immorality—vices in real life the college censor saw in Joyce's essay and in fiction that the president of the college fears in his dialogue with Stephen in *Hero*. By contrast, Joyce saw that these very issues required liberating expression in literature through the unorthodox religious texts he cites. The writer of the editorial goes on to caution Joyce against the very thing Joyce most sought to do: "If Mr. Joyce thinks that the artist must stand apart from the multitude, and means that he must sever himself from the moral and religious teachings which have, under Divine guidance, molded its spiritual character, we join issue against him."[19] Joyce does stand apart, his fellow students against him, and the verb "sever" is the key to it all. To sever oneself from the Catholic point of view is for the Irish nationalists damning and excommunicatory, but to sever oneself from that institution is, for Joyce, to be liberated from a mediated "guidance," less divine than authoritative. Severing is another way of tearing, of opening up possibilities in schism free from the nationalist mentality that allowed dogma to construct and constrict its identity.

To stand against this monolith of culture allied with Catholicism, Joyce offers up in "Rabblement" the usual pan-European literary suspects: Flaubert, Tolstoy, Hauptmann, D'Annunzio (the first and last of these, renegade Catholics). Yet that previous year in his essays and later in *Hero* Joyce finds a hidden and more powerful counterstance to Irish mediocrity in Protestant texts. With them he can break the complicity of church and culture.

The tensions Joyce felt at University College, as indicated in his essay on the "Rabblement" and the response it received from fellow students and clerical authorities, are expressed fully in *Stephen Hero*. Initially, Joyce appeared to *need* to write fully about these tensions and constraints, as well as about his engagement with Protestant ideas and texts. But he came to both a psychological and critical assessment: having written much of *Hero* and at great length, he could move beyond its detailed treatment of the attitudes of his college days and condense the features of his *Bildung* into the more poignant and immediate narrative of *Portrait*. In *Hero* we find an illustration of Joyce's contrarian break with the church far more explicit than the one in *Portrait*. Moreover, just as *Hero* is the original text of the Joycean nexus of religious rebellion and Protestant attraction, so too it adds to the mix the resistance to nationalism. These issues are all connected, in a narrative not known for its economy, within the brief span of a conversation about Madden's fervent wish to liberate himself from political oppression, a move Stephen thinks would not be desirable. The third-person narration informs the reader of Stephen's reasoning: "The Roman, not the Sassenach, was for [Stephen] the tyrant of the islanders. . . . The watchcry was Faith and Fatherland" (*SH* 53). Early on in Joyce's writing career, then, he makes clear his conviction that a very particular oppression would remain to Ireland even when the shackles of imperialism were thrown off: an oppression combining church and culture. (Joyce reasserts the validity of this claim later in "Saints and Sages" in 1907.) And, as if to make the final connection of all the issues Joyce felt impinged upon his freedom, in this demand for faithful submission Joyce inevitably saw implicated the language question. Stephen says that the priests "encourage the study of Irish that their flocks may be more safely protected from the <<wolves of disbelief>>" (*SH* 54, critical marks in the text). While in the immediate context the wolves of disbelief are the processes of modernity that the church fears for its faithful—the attractions of the material world and the licentiousness of literature—they are also the challenges to faith issuing from the English language itself. To Madden's claim that "the peasant has nothing to gain from English Literature" (its capitalization indicating its status as an academic subject), Stephen's reply shows how easily he moves between Britain and Europe: "English is the medium for the Continent." It is undeniably true that the appeal of the Continent was strong in Joyce's literary life (as well as in his actual life in exile), but it is striking to see how the magical Continent that so strongly attracted him connects so clearly for him with England and its literature. Joyce may well have wanted to live abroad, but he knew that real freedom of expression, freedom from church dogma and nationalist unreality, would come to him through the English language. That is the main reason for Joyce's attention to the literary attractions of Protestantism in the Authorized Version and the prayer book. That interest continues long after Joyce has left Ireland behind.

*Hero*, then, has its position in Joyce's evolving schismatic turn, with its explicit engagement with Protestantism following soon after he defined the stories in *Dubliners* as "epicleti." The appeal to Protestantism is set out precisely as a challenge to Rome and to Tara. By entertaining that transfer of loyalty, Joyce engages in an act of apostasy that would, certainly, have run counter to the grain of his teachers and forebears at UCD, the arena of what is extant in *Hero*. Newman, most illustriously, and the dean of studies, more humbly, were converts of the Oxford Movement from Canterbury to Rome. Swimming always against the tide of religion and culture, Stephen in *Hero* actually entertains the attractions of Protestantism. *Portrait* obscures this interest; its narrative line functions clearly as a rejection of the Catholic Church without Stephen's ever actually considering Protestantism; indeed, his rejection of Rome proceeds without any alternatives other than his own freedom. We have seen, however, that Joyce conceives of that freedom as necessarily engaged through schism, by finding a place to break with the dominance of Catholicism in culture and language.

One particular passage in *Portrait* that addresses the measure of Protestantism is often cited as definitive of Joyce's view (although we have already demonstrated that Joyce's interest in such ideas continues throughout his career and into the *Wake*). With Cranly, Stephen has a long discussion of the power of the Eucharist—the very issue at stake in the turning of the *Dubliners* stories by epiclesis into consubstantial narrative figures rather than real presences. (The importance of this passage for its schismatic misbelief is crucial, because it turns from Catholicism to Protestantism, and it is modeled on real life. This passage is clearly a fictional account of James' and Stanislaus' conversation described in *My Brother's Keeper* and discussed in the previous chapter.) Probing Stephen's unwillingness to take communion, Cranly conjectures that is "because you feel that the host too may be the body and blood of the son of God and not a wafer of bread? And because you fear it may be?" Stephen answers, "I feel that and I fear it." Cranly seeks to define that fear: "the God of the roman catholics would strike you dead and damn you if you made a sacrilegious communion?" "I fear more," said Stephen, "the chemical action which would be set up in my soul by a false homage to a symbol behind which are massed twenty centuries of authority and veneration " (*P* 243). The issue here, as always, for Stephen is fidelity to his own thinking, the integrity of the choice guiding the ideals he holds and those he rejects. This sense of integrity is the reason Joyce is so concerned with the schismatic, which necessitates both choice and rejection. Moreover, this necessity only underscores (again) the fact that the idea held or the concept rejected is important as an idea: religion is an intellectual construct, not of faith but of ideation, and faithfulness is finally a construct of one's own mind.

Cranly clearly touches on the difficult issue of transubstantiation when he nominates the "god of the roman catholics" the God of the Real Presence and then questions whether Stephen could view the host as figurative: "you do not intend to become a protestant?" To this Stephen gives the clever answer that sums up his attitude to the Western Schism: "I said that I had lost my faith . . . but not my selfrespect. What kind of liberation would that be to forsake an absurdity which is logical and coherent and to embrace one that is illogical and incoherent?" (*P* 244). Stephen's answer demonstrates pride in the intellectual imagination, in apostasy as idea; it has the cleverness of a Wildean paradox in the service of the theological paradox of the Eucharist. It also takes a very modern, scientific analytical turn in its mention of a chemical (that is, corrosive) action in the soul. Stephen seems to dismiss Protestantism as sloppy, because illogical. After all, it is the intellectual attraction of theological ideas that draws Joyce into concern for religion and for the possibilities offered by schismatic intellectual stands. Through Stephen, Joyce dismisses Protestantism on the ground that it is not rigorous in idea. All matters of faith, all practices of worship (although these, too, will come under scrutiny) appear less consequential when contrasted to the attraction of logical thought. Yet there is always something diversionary in any Joycean assertion. Illogical Protestantism might be, but it has its schismatic attractions.

Surely the Joyce who would take the time to transcribe Revelation would have purposes not so clearly dismissible by an epigram such as *Portrait* provides above. In *Stephen Hero* the titular character shows a repeated interest in Protestantism that more closely parallels Joyce's actual explorations of and challenges to his upbringing and education than does the Stephen of *Portrait*. *Portrait*'s epigrammatic sentence at best demonstrates that Joyce's choice for freedom was to be his alone, although the means by which he would make it would rely on many sources.

The indirect discourse of *Hero* permits a greater imposition of authorial judgment than does the narrative of *Portrait*. An example of such influence occurs in the observation that even when Stephen "has been a Roman Catholic in the proper sense of the term, the figure of Jesus seemed to him too remote" (*SH* 11) and he prayed rather to Mary as his intercessor. The intermediate mode of his "proper" Catholic worship occurs through others, much as religious authority comes from the priests' mediation of the Word rather than through Stephen's own direct reading of it. Yet Stephen grows away from the church: his "enfranchisement from the discipline of the church seemed to be coincident with a natural instinctive return to the Founder thereof and this impulse would have led him perhaps to a consideration of the merits of Protestantism" (*SH* 112). Here is an attack on the mode of worship rather than on its intellectual framework, and two of those likely "merits" he actually engages are the reading of scripture for personal enlightenment and the challenging of proper authority through such reading. The chain of conditions indicated in the phrasing "would have led . . . perhaps . . . to a consideration" represents an infinitely postponed act, a prolegomena of apostasy whose evident attractions of freedom and personal authority remain always possible in some future time.

As the previous chapter makes clear, a major part of Joyce's thought about art leans toward the schismatic of Protestantism: to consider the Eucharist an analogy for art is to deny the Real Presence in transubstantiation with the consequence that making it metaphoric thus approaches consubstantiation. The issue in both *Hero* and *Portrait* between Catholicism and Protestantism is one of liberation. It is certainly odd to think that religion (Protestant or any other) would be regarded by an artist as a route to liberation; the artist of the late nineteenth century would be apt to find all beliefs constricting. With his contrarian impulse, Joyce always wished to position himself as a schismatic, searching for the place where orthodoxy cracks and the "other" approaches. At the beginning of his writing career, he copies out the ultimate end, transcribing the Protestant Revelation of Saint John but giving it the Catholic title, Apocalypse—a literary version of having his cake and eating it too.

Joyce was attracted to whatever order he did not belong to, even though he was suspicious of those to which he did belong, for to be so attracted was to be in a position of choosing to be free from control, to rend authority, to be in constant schismatic motion. Protestantism appealed to Joyce because, as a religion, it made no claim on him. In this double exchange of loyalty and rebellion, he could be fascinated by individuals who rejected the unrigorous latitudinarianism and logical laxity of Anglicanism to voluntarily adopt the strictures of Rome from which he sought to break.

One way to see Joyce's contrarian fascination is not only in the Catholic-born Stephen's interest in Protestantism, but also in the turn-again quality of other characters in *Portrait* who, though Protestant-born, are interested in Catholicism. If Joyce does not closely pursue Stephen's flirtation with Protestantism in that novel, traces of it remain by suggestive opposition in these problematic figures. The English converts of the Oxford Movement are a set of those who "together turn" (literally "con-vertere"), schismatics who voluntarily leave their dominant religion to embrace the faith that constrains the Irish. They represent for Stephen, as for Joyce, the actuality of a reversed but incomplete break; what they might have gained from their schism, Joyce and Stephen feel, is lost in their embrace of another institutional religion.

The presence of the Oxford Movement clergy in Ireland was due no doubt to the congenial Catholic environment of a country still in the union and whose language was the same, but whose numerically dominant faithful offered far greater opportunities for employment and engagement. Two figures, one foregrounded in the text, the other more implicitly drawn, are a crucial if contrasting part of the narrative of Stephen's apostasy. The first is the dean of studies in *Portrait*, of whose conversion Stephen remarks in terms that suggest its double nature. (See chapters 1 and 2 for a full discussion of Stephen's view of the dean.) The second is Father Butt of *Hero*, a prototype of the dean. One of the actual persons who was the model for these fictional representations was Father Joseph Darlington, one of Joyce's instructors at University College, who, Ellmann notes, was "an English convert."[20] So was Thomas Arnold, his colleague in the English faculty. (Thomas Arnold, brother of Matthew Arnold, and son of Thomas of Rugby, turned from his long Anglican lineage and, remarkably, was converted twice.) Ellmann suggests that Joyce had a strong "scorn for Darlington" and attributes it to Darlington's belief that Joyce could sell his talent. Apparently Darlington suggested to Joyce that he write as a sideline to a respectable profession such as the law.[21] Another likely source of Stephen (and Joyce's) disdain might well be their view of the apostasy of Darlington, the fact that he was (finally) a convert to Catholicism. To maintain the freedom of schism, Joyce knew, one must remain attracted to the opposite but never to embrace it, as the act of acceptance would cancel out all the benefits of the opposition. To hold to schism was to be both and neither. To go over wholeheartedly to the other side was, finally, to be a turncoat and, as such, an object of disdain.

The famous passage about language, in which Stephen feels at once a part of the dean's speech and also alien from it, is in one way a version of the sliding frame of apostasy the two characters represent: one schismatically dropping away from the true faith, the other voluntarily embracing it. The tension between the two characters is a fruitful way to combine orthodoxy and rebellion. In the language they both speak, Stephen feels an "unrest of spirit" as his "soul frets in the shadow" of the words (P 189). Those terms—"spirit," "soul," and "shadow"—come more readily from religious than from daily usage, and their appearance in that literary context indicates the mediated ground between the two figures who are practicing apostasy and schism from their particular backgrounds. To be familiar is to be part of what one has grown up with, be it religion or a mother tongue. To be foreign is to move to some distance toward something else, similar but not wholly the same. To speak with someone who has adopted what you reject, who has turned from one religion to another, is to stand together in a place of alienating possibilities and openness of meaning. Stephen's arch quotation about "sitting at receipt of custom" shares that mediating quality, as it straddles the language of both the Authorized Protestant Bible and the Catholic English one.

That mediating space between the dean of studies and Stephen is indicated again the oblique presentation of the rector of Belvedere in *Portrait*, an unnamed figure based on the real-life Father William Henry. Unremarked in the text is the real-life Henry's identity as a convert of the Oxford Movement. Stanislaus harshly calls Father Henry "a fanatical convert from Protestantism."[22] Sullivan presents a more balanced assessment, suggesting that Henry was rather fond of Joyce for his intelligence and must have felt benignly enough toward him to allow Joyce the license to mock him at the Whitsun play.[23] While his conversion does not receive overt representation in *Portrait*, it does appear obliquely in the very quotation which serves as the text of Stephen's parody: "let him be to thee a heathen." We have noted that this line, quoted by Eck to Luther in the Wittenberg hearing, informs the historical context of the Western Schism. It also intentionally mediates between the Catholic and Anglican bibles. The rector, whose sonorous delivery of the line Stephen parodies in the school play, is himself a mixture of the Protestant and the Catholic, someone fallen away from his native church to lead in the other.

Of course, the largest figure of conversion from Protestantism to Catholicism for the whole of the culture was John Henry, Cardinal Newman. The appeal of Newman's prose to Stephen in chapters 3 and 4 of *Portrait* might be seen as another way of his assimilating the language issue raised by his conversation with the dean of studies. In chapter 4, the preuniversity Stephen reflects twice on Newman. He remembers the image of "the feet of harts" (165) which, for Joyce, figures always the beleaguered independent soul. It is an image Stephen uses for himself in *Hero*—as a stag "flashing his antlers"(35)—and for the fallen Parnell in the poem in "Ivy Day in the Committee Room." Newman's conversion thus seems of a piece with a heroic act of rebellion. That the "let him be to thee a heathen" line appears in Newman's "The Idea of a University" connects him with the scene between Stephen and the dean of students, which takes place in a lecture hall of University College that Newman helped to found. A scene earlier, Stephen thinks of the destitution of his family by recalling Newman's response to a line from Virgil in "The Grammar of Assent" (*P* 164). The Newman citation strengthens and deepens Stephen's account of his home life. Insofar as Newman's argument in "Assent" is that rhetorical commonplaces in Virgil are most meaningful to mature readers rather than to schoolboys, Joyce makes himself something greater by the allusion. (One might suggest along the same lines that biblical commonplaces such as "my right hand loses its cunning" from the Authorized Version are most meaningful when used by a young Catholic writer.) The other mention of Newman comes earlier in *Portrait*, but at a crucial juncture which this study foregrounds: the passage where Heron accuses Byron of heresy. Asked who is the best prose writer, Stephen names Newman—a claim to which Stephen's tormentors agree. Nevertheless, the scene still ends with the "torn" Stephen a martyr to his beliefs in an oblique presentation of the perils and possibilities of the schismatic stand.

Allusions to Newman allow Joyce to maintain his alternating position between the contradictions and attractions of the Anglican converts.[24] He can as easily disdain the Protestant cause as he can the Darlingtons who leave it for the Catholic Church. The president of the college in *Hero* seeks to censor Stephen's essay on drama; in their interview, several issues raised by such conversions come together—rebellion, faith, culture, and literature. Concerned by the content of Stephen's paper about drama and worried about Stephen's increasing interest in secular culture, the president seeks to dissuade Stephen from his interest in Ibsen. Ibsen is always for Joyce the figure of the great contrarian, and Stephen is eager to defend Ibsen's disdain for the conventions of society and art. His defense is clever, appealing to the president through the sainted Cardinal Newman and his dislike of the Protestant middle class: "I mean that Ibsen's account of modern society is as genuinely ironical as Newman's account of English Protestant morality and belief" (*SH* 92). Stephen must think that this line of argument will be unfailing with the president, appealing as it does to his own prejudice against Protestants. The president notes with some satisfaction that when Newman spoke, the effect was devastating on the defender of Anglican faith, "Poor Kingsley." Stephen is quite willing to use Newman's position against Protestant thinking as an example of contrarianism that is the fruit of schism, even though Newman in another way comes to represent the very constraints that Catholicism places on Stephen, especially as the president seeks to censure his essay and his reading.

This pressure becomes apparent when the president stays with the very questions of propriety that Stephen wants to escape. The president talks of Ibsen being like Zola, that bugbear of a lapsed Catholic who represents the forbidden quality of art that must be censured by the *Index*. He does so in unmistakable terms of religious thought: Ibsen was "like Zola with some new kind of doctrine to preach . . . a social doctrine, free living, unbridled license" (*SH* 93).[25] The irony of Stephen's use of the convert Newman to justify his interest in Ibsen, his balancing one form of schism with another form of rebellion to keep all freedom in play, forces him up against the constraints of his religion. The confines of propriety (Ibsen, the president claims, cannot be named "even in mixed company"), the fear of freedom, the openness of realism—in short, everything Joyce sought to find by means of his schismatic self-positioning—is foreclosed by the president in the name of Catholic orthodoxy. While the presentation of Anglican converts in his work proves a fruitful avenue for Joyce's testing the limits of orthodoxy, within the context of Catholicism where he stands, all such moves are to little avail. Not even citing Newman will break the strictures of the church against anything open and liberating. Only Joyce's maintaining a schismatic stance will do that.

The president's fear of "license" and topics that cannot be named "even in mixed company" marks the church's prudery about real-life issues, a prudery Joyce found so very vexing. To run from the church's authority was also to escape its reticence on sexual matters. Unconstrained, he could choose his subjects at will; he could voice the urgent matters that the church met with silence.

If Joyce found the Catholic Church unattractive precisely for its monolithic authority and rigidity, he most particularly resisted the church's obtuse silence about issues of real life: its unwillingness to acknowledge the forces within human beings and the forces in the surrounding culture that spoke to their drives and needs. Even as late at the 1930s, as one study shows, young Catholic men and women were wholly unprepared by the church about sex in marriage: "most brides entered married life with an incredible naiveté about sexual matters," because, "for the most part, the subject [of sex] was taboo."[26] The legacy continued for a half century more: Dubliners were frequently ignorant and ill at ease about sex due to their "reliance upon the teaching powers of the Church as voiced by the clergy" and even into the 1960s "the Church dominated the field of Irish sexuality [and it] tended not to be discussed."[27] To combat its constraint and repression, Joyce favored the very physical remedy proposed in "The Holy Office" of 1905, that of the cathartic purgative. He consistently demanded frankness, resisting the church's way of idealizing, even etherealizing human drives. In a famous letter in which he discusses the "sexual department" of his "soul's well," he confesses to needing a purge himself: "I am nauseated about [the church's] lying drivel about pure men and pure women, . . . lying in the face of truth" (*Letters* 2:191–92). In the essay "Drama and Life," which we have seen is concerned with a new way in literature, he urged what he called the actual, "men and women as we meet them in the real world" (*CW* 45), not "altered by religious . . . and idealising tendencies" (44). For Joyce, to idealize was to avoid and omit; the church, as it could not refine needs and desires out of existence, would chose not to speak of them at all. Schism could tear down the idealization by breaking open the silence.

There was also a native authority exerting similar constraint and silence from which he likewise sought to escape, that of Irish nationalism. It meshed too closely with the church, not only in its call to service, but in its reticence about real life. As Joyce remarked in the same letter about the church's nauseating idealizations, nationalism also sought to sanitize the drives of its own citizens. He mocked the periodical *Sinn Fein* for its use of the phrase "venereal excess" when simple sexuality was its subject (*Letters* 2:191). In this context so important to Joyce, the realist who expressed the drives and needs of actual beings in an actual world, nationalism supported the church's silence.

So, to resist the church first and the nationalism that supported it secondarily, Joyce looked elsewhere. Frank and open discussion of sexuality challenged the Catholic Church's silence and prudery; it was also at odds with Irish culture which, although once bawdy and lively, had been so subjugated by the church that it had become ignorant and ashamed. (Joyce declaims in "Saints and Sages" against the "frigid enthusiast, sexually and artistically untaught" [*CW* 173].)[28]

Any religion that would enable Joyce to talk about the way human beings live in the real world would have an attraction for him; that such a religion additionally would be, from the Catholic view, schismatic, would make it nearly irresistible. With it he could speak in unidealized terms about what motivates real human beings without falling back on a moral scheme that would actually suppress what is most true to human experience. With that other religion he could say things that were taboo to Rome and to Tara: he could talk about sex, and about money, and about sex and money.

That religion most clearly "other" and most readily at hand was Protestantism. Although it seems anomalous that the Anglican Church in Ireland—highly conventional, somnolent even—would appear liberating and open, it was so only in contrast to the heavy weight of Rome. But it also had the advantage of running against fervent Celticism. As Protestantism was tied to England, Joyce could make a dig at Irish nationalism at the same time he critiqued the Irish Catholic Church. Moreover, to talk about issues of sex and money was to address the sources of actual power in the real world, sources that command the most effective obedience and dominance. What license Protestantism offered Joyce was the opportunity to talk about issues that actually drove the modern world, primarily imperial and capitalist Britain.

What English culture and Protestant liturgy afforded Joyce was a language of the actual, where sexuality and power and money were affirmed as forces dominant and right in human experience. If to discuss sexuality at all would be a challenge to the Roman Church and the Irish nation, to speak of it in terms of Protestant ideology and English culture would be a consistent and logical schismatic challenge.

The crucial domain wherein the "other" and freedom conjoin is sexuality, which for Joyce was the essential reality of human and artistic activity. For Joyce, sexuality offered individual liberation and openness against which the church was firmly set, as evidenced in *Hero* in the president's prudery about Zola and Ibsen. In *Hero*, the sexual attractions of women are made quite clear, while in *Portrait* women function primarily as distant, aesthetic objects. Because Stephen's and Lynch's frankness about the attractions of women and the possibilities of their seduction is a subject unspoken in Catholic life, it must be expressed in *Hero* in terms of Protestant liturgy.

Discussing Stephen's shocking request to Emma that they "lie together," Lynch suggests that, in contrast, proposing marriage would be "relatively sane." Stephen disagrees, asking "Have you ever read the Form of Solemnization of Marriage in the *Book of Common Prayer*?" (*Hero* 201)[29] To Lynch's negative, Stephen suggests he should and goes on to assert that while Lynch's "everyday life is Protestant," when he discusses things he "shows himself a Catholic," apparently in the logic of his responses. Stephen then notes the grounds of his claim for the insanity of marriage and the inadequacies of the Anglican prayer book: "A man who swears to love a woman till death part him and her is sane neither in the opinion of the philosopher who understands what mutability is nor in the opinion of the man of the world who understands that it is safer to be a witness than an actor in such affairs. A man who swears to do something which is not in his power to do is not accounted a sane man" (*SH* 201). The very claim in question, "forsaking all others, keep[ing] thee only to her, as long as ye both shall live" is found only in the Protestant service. So the foremost issue for Stephen is, as with the logic of Catholicism over Protestantism, the fidelity not of man to woman but fidelity to the logical choice one might make under an oath. Again, Stephen appears to be concerned with the rigor of his thinking, but surely his invitation to Emma to lie with him is an opening to the sexuality that undergirds the act of marriage. While Stephen suggests that a sexual relationship with Emma outside marriage is a sensible choice in a mutable world, one that does not require consistency (and also a choice that would identify him a freethinking person), he frames his entire discussion around the sexual invitation. Even to connect sexuality with the Anglican liturgy is to suggest that, for the Protestant other, marriage speaks to sexuality in a way in which the Catholic Church remains silent. And the attraction of sexuality is foregrounded in the words of the very same Anglican service he mentions.

In the odd ways in which a schismatic turn makes other religions attractive, the Book of Common Prayer for Joyce becomes a guide to sexual seduction. Enjoining that marriage is not to be entered into "to satisfy men's carnal lusts and appetites," but is ordained "for a remedy . . . that such persons as have not the gift of continency," the Anglican prayer book fully acknowledges the sex drive. Where the Roman prayer book will not speak of sexuality at all, the Anglican one openly announces it.[30] And even if hedged by proscriptions, the service *does* acknowledge the physical rites of marriage: the groom, while pledging the ring, says, "with my body I thee worship." This is a strikingly frank admission of the sexual realities of marriage and of the bride as the object of desire for which the marriage ceremony is a social solemnization.[31] Desire is every man's object, even if in his particular culture he must cite the prayer book of another religion to express it. (In this context we should remember that Heron uses the spiritual term "oracle" as his secret word for sexual activity.) The transgressive attraction of reading and thinking about sex, and Stephen's socially shocking if not actually transgressive request of Emma, are made equal to and possible by Stephen's citation from the prayer book of the schismatic (and hegemonic) Anglican Church. What he asks of Emma is shocking to his church and his culture; what he reads and cites is the same.

This frank expression of the sex drive by the Anglican prayer book continues to appeal to Joyce. Never one to leave an idea alone, and always consistent in his rebellious choices, Joyce returns to the vows from the solemnization of marriage in *Ulysses*. While no longer personally constrained by the church and Ireland, Joyce continues to exercise his schismatic impulses by showing his characters' similar quests to liberate themselves through the unlikely adoption of a religiously rebellious otherness. The issues of sexuality, shame, and marriage as the legitimization of desire all recur in "Circe" when Bloom imagines encountering Gerty McDowell. Now added to them in the materialist matrix of *Ulysses* is expression of another desire forbidden by Rome: the desire to acquire wealth. As the flawed girl *"limps forward"* and shows Bloom something private and shameful, the "bloody clouts" of her menstruation, she says, "With all my worldly goods I thee and thou. . . . You did that. . . . Dirty married man!" (15.372–85). Gerty's physical limitations (her limp, her menstruating) are shameful, as is her economic condition. All this is served by her citing, or Bloom's imagining her citing, from the Anglican solemnization of marriage. For Gerty, marriage is the socially acceptable structure that, in her thoughts, admits of no sexual component (as when she daydreams of marriage consisting, in its physical manifestation, as the toast rack on sale at Cleary's). For her, as an unmarried older girl, marriage is an economic support system, not a system of mediated desire and sexual gratification, and that understanding is nowhere better illustrated than in her pledge of "worldly goods." She mis-quotes the entire phrase from the prayer book—"with all my worldly goods I thee endow"—quite conspicuously leaving out the verb "endow" as she has no goods to gift. Instead, she revises the phrase as a self-and-other series: "I thee and thou." Moreover, the pledge of "worldly goods" is made by the man to the woman, so Gerty, in her wishes, overturns gender roles. Yet for this she too requires words from the Anglican marriage service (as did the Stephen of *Hero*) to express what she seeks in the marriage state, the satisfaction of her financial needs and desires. It is Protestantism, that religious and schismatic other, which provides the advantage to address the real issue of marriage as a financial contract, a real view that the Catholic Church obscures. For Gerty, if Bloom is a Protestant "it wouldn't matter," but surely for Joyce, as it is for the Stephen in *Hero*, it matters a great deal to be able to cite from an Anglican text.

To admit the attraction of sex and money is to admit their power, and to acknowledge their power is to confess that they constitute real effective influ-ence in the world as irresistible and dominant natural forces in contrast to the empty idealizations offered by the Catholic Church and Irish nationalism. The openness made possible by phrases from the marriage service in the Anglican prayer book persists into *Finnegans Wake*, even though Joyce no longer has to battle any institutional authority. *Finnegans Wake* was produced at a time when another Ireland had come to be. Against the wishes of the nationalists, the country was partitioned, but much to the gratification of the church, it was wedded closely to Rome. Joyce summed up this anomaly of the new divided and religious Ireland with reference again to a phrase from the Anglican mar-riage service: "And though dev do espart" (626.31). In the *Wake* the very use of the Book of Common Prayer is Joyce's acknowledgment of the efficacy of a power based on the acknowledgment of sex and money; the dominant imperial modern culture brings all that in its train.

The possibilities afforded Joyce by an appeal to Protestantism early in his career and in his flight from home and church go hand in hand with the later openness of the *Wake* to all sorts of challenging choices. In that text, there is no single authority, so the attractions of the religious other are widespread through it. The Koran is as likely a source of expressions otherness as the Angli-can prayer book. The substitutionality in the *Wake* seems to be rather the point: the claim of the authority of the Catholic Church and of nationhood is seri-ously compromised. This substitutionality is the last of Joyce's challenges to the magisterium he had left behind long before; he is consistent to his schismatic impulse. Yet if the Roman Church is no longer an overwhelming force in Joyce's life, issues of sexuality, economics, and power certainly are. In the multiphonic otherness of the *Wake*, Joyce still makes recourse to Protestantism to express those topics he called "real life" thirty years earlier. All the following passages from the *Wake* show Joyce's persistent conflation of marriage with sex, money, and masculine power—issues never spoken by the mother church but essential to British and Protestant effectiveness.

The invaluable Clive Hart finds in the *Wake* some twenty-seven leitmotif echoes of the marriage vows from the Book of Common Prayer.[32] Take as an example this brief passage from the end of book 3, chapter 3, where Earwicker defends himself by asserting his bona fides as both citizen and husband in religious terms. He claims, with some hesitancy, the validity of his "dudud dirtynine articles" (534.12) which, whatever their pornographic faults, are the substance of an Anglican identity. That identity, in turn, legitimates his claim to Dublin and the Liffey, as the conquering Norseman and Norman. Conquest and dominance go along with the book of the English Church. Through imagery of boating—the invader's means of access—his conquest and treatment of ALP emerge in unequivocally sexual terms: "by wavebrink . . . with mace to masthigh, did I upreized my magicianer's puntpole" (547.24). Conquering the river as alien Norseman and Norman—"I abridged with domfine norseman-ship"—he can claim his sexual rights—"I had done abate her maidan race, my baresark bride, and knew her fleshly"—where the naked bride is like an open ark (of the covenant and of Noah). This conquest of land and bride, moreover, takes place within the context of a sexuality condoned by rite, the same rite Stephen obliquely cites in *Hero* in the phrase, "with all my bawdy did I her whorship." (574.29) Here the words of the Anglican marriage service recur. The emphasis on sexuality evidenced in the wordplay of "bawdy" for "body" and "whorship" for "worship" makes clear the parallel between marriage as sacramental "worship" and prostitution for money. Joyce's manipulation of the Anglican marriage service to refer obliquely to marriage's sexual component in *Hero* and to its economic dimensions in *Ulysses*, culminates in the *Wake* in bombastic claims of paternal conquest and dominance.

The conflation of marriage and power through articulations of the Protestant other continues into the domestic scenes of the Porters in book 3, episode 4. By making Porter specifically an "episcopalian," and his wife a member of the Scottish "free-kirk" (559.26), Joyce enjoys tweaking the unity of Anglicanism with a little sectarian nationalism. The loyalty promoted in the thirty-nine articles is elided in reference to thirty-nine sex positions (with a glance at the Kama Sutra), and the marriage is challenged by a divorce proceeding (very English and Reformation Protestant), with its social concerns about money and power, a question of "the payment of tithes" (574.89), and a question of whether the husband "has he hegemony and shall she submit" (573.32). It is not surprising that this exchange is played out as a case between the churches of Rome and England, represented as two economic and legal firms, "Brerfuchs and Warren, since disseized" and "Tangos, Limited." In the battle between Rome and England, Joyce comes down on the side of the other, because it has always had the attraction of allowing him to speak of these powers in the real world.

In all, Protestantism appealed to Joyce without commanding his obedience (in truth, it had little authority with which to command); even if illogical in some of its positions, it was an established order, not Joyce's own, affording him a rebellious authority with no strings attached. By occupying a schismatic position, Joyce could reject Catholicism while using, but not adhering to, another system, one particularly at odds with Rome in his country and his culture.

Yet perhaps the surest way for Joyce to break with Rome's hegemony without submitting to its weaker opposite in Canterbury was to embrace both positions, and more. To hold contrary positions was to be a true misbeliever and derive great freedom by challenging unitary meaning and sliding always into the space opened by schism. *Finnegans Wake* may well be the quintessential text for acknowledging all orders equally, giving room to all and pride of place to none. The references to and echoes of other religious texts, scriptural and liturgical, make this point convincingly. Throughout the *Wake*, no matter the context, there are phrases that clearly signal religious texts. The Egyptian Book of the Dead is as likely a source of expression as the Anglican burial service. Catholic vernacular worship supplies scriptural references as do Anglican sources.[33] Vernacular worship by itself is a challenge to pastoral and papal authority (with Catholic worship in English as a slap at the absurdity of Gaelic linguistic purity through Latin liturgy). In many instances, scriptures are the same in both Catholic and Protestant worship. This being the case, the claim of there being one true church is seriously compromised. Thus, the very means of alluding to a text not explicitly Protestant but ambivalently both Protestant and Catholic puts a particular emphasis on the freedom and possibility offered by the religious other.[34]

One example is the Pater Noster, which Hart finds referenced some thirty-six times.[35] What can be said of this prayer can be said of nearly any echo in the *Wake*—that it performs in a multiplicity of ways to support the manifold purposes of the work. The prayer returns, in capsule form, to the issues of sex and power Joyce saw as real and effective. Patriarchy is clearly underscored by the associations drawn between the prayer and HCE's identity as conqueror: "our kingable kahn" (32.02); "Foughtarundser" (78.16). Earwicker is part of an economic context: "Harrod's be the naun . . . mine wohl be won" (536.34). His weaknesses are also made manifest: he is the "pesternost" (596.10); "Panther monster" (244.34); "farternoiser" (530.36). His sins, too, are prominent: "forbids us our trespassers" (128.34) signals his transgressions against property and ownership, while "forgiver of trosstpassers" (345.28) signals his failure to keep his oaths. Even ALP comes in for this veneration: "haloed be her eve; her singtime sung" (104.14) Joyce's immediate purpose is to challenge the assumptions about the gender of divinity, creating a "Maternostra" alongside his "Mamafesta." HCE's generosity also extends incestuously to his daughter, "Oscarvaughter" (326.07).

The Lord's Prayer was common both to Catholic and Protestant vernacular worship; to cite it is to bring both religions into play in a manner similar to bringing both sexes together. Both are present and neither is dominant. Similarly, phrasings from vernacular worship common to both observances are transformed in the *Wake* to speak to various purposes and themes: "Let us pray"; "pray for us"; and "peace be with them." "Let us pray" can appear in the Latin as "oremus" (398.12) and "Oremus" (489.06), but it also appears differently, as "orimis" (418.05). The slip between "e" and "i" suggests the small variations in quotations between the Douay and Authorized bibles, a slip (or break) that opens up possibilities of schism. The phrase can also serve other purposes: in "Oremunds" (105.02), orality is stressed; in "O'remus" (122.09), ethnic variety is indicated by reference to an Irish surname and an American storyteller. In a text filled with suspicion and secrecy, there is the imperative "let us pry" (188.08); and in a text famed for verbal instability, there is "letters play" (237.08). As both Catholics and Protestants worship differently with similar words, so the worship of the same and the other can admit the likeness of others: "let outers play" (482.19). Rephrased, "Pray for us" as "Playfulness" (601.22) can become a joke; a request to a pagan deity, "Hora Pro Nubis" (514.22); or the bonding with a community, "ara poog neighbors" (492.12). This last phrase embeds the popular work of Dion Boucicault, *Arrah-na-Pogue*, as part of a bonding process similar to that implied by prayer. The common culture of prayer and popular literature is a point to which Joyce turns often in these allusions, as the combination constitutes a most powerful argument about the limitations of the Catholic Church. "Peace be with them," appropriately for a work with strong Irish connections, becomes "peats be with them" (202.30)—a common touch, of the earth, earthy.

While it is incontestable that these phrases have passed into common parlance and exist at the level of cliché, Joyce was, without question, aware of their origins in worship and delighted to see that they had passed into the vernacular culture. By becoming catchphrases, their power as responses in dogmatic belief is greatly lessened, a devolution that would have appealed to Joyce in his wish to diminish the power of the church. Along with this diminution in the majesty of worship dictated by the magisterium, was, particularly for Joyce, the sense that when such phrases are used equally by Protestants and Catholics—on Sundays in church and on weekdays in the marketplace—neither can claim to be sole arbiter of the faith, nor can the language itself be sanitized of the realities of actual life. Common phrases of worship belong to various altars, some of them schismatic, and also to the marketplace in the real world to which Joyce was himself so faithful. Though truth, Joyce averred, exists, it represents only about "ten percent of the truth," comprised of broken phrases disrupted by schismatic pressures.[36] In *Portrait*, the noble and elevated dialogue between the dean of studies and Stephen about the native power of words is narrowed and restricted by Stephen's playful use of the word "detain" to trip up his interlocutor. The too-easy pun, challenging authority as did the Whitsuntide play, allows Stephen to remark on difference: "One difficulty . . . in esthetic discussion is to know whether words are used according to the literary tradition or according to the tradition of the marketplace" (*P* 188). In the spaces of schism, between the dean's conversion and Stephen's resistance, lies a space between alternatives; similarly in the space between *traditio*—as much religious as literary—and the real world is an area of choice and rebellion. The pun operates both early and late to accommodate that openness.

Nevertheless, while English phrases common to the worship of both Catholics and Anglicans are present in the *Wake* to undermine authoritative claims of the church of Joyce's upbringing, there are also phrases that come particularly from forms of Anglican worship, particularly the Book of Common Prayer.[37] The *Wake*, for all its universality and perhaps because of it, maintains English as the universal language and consequently also embraces an English culture of power and reality that for Joyce resisted religious and ethnic claims to universality.

The Great Litany for Lent is a prayer of public intercession whose theme of sin and forgiveness is crucial to the *Wake* and whose intercessory method is crucial to the *Wake*'s aural structure. The repeated "hear us, we beseech thee, O Lord," Joyce transforms as "Loud we beseech thee" and "Loud hear us," where volume replaces divinity (in a most inefficacious manner) to arrive at the confused and mortal state of being heard *and* distressed: "Loud heap miseries upon us." Another striking and now-common phrase—"the world, the flesh, and the devil"—appears in the first section of the Litany, the deprecations for deliverance: "from fornication and all other deadly sin; and from all the deceits of the world, the flesh, and the devil, // Good Lord, deliver us." This request demonstrates the sexual frankness that Joyce found in the Protestant marriage solemnization. In the *Wake*, the phrase becomes part of something dynamic, "the whirl, the flash, and the trouble" (220.28), whose fragmentary motion enacts the sexual attraction and the costs that lie behind the children's games at the start of 1.3. Similarly, "the wittol, the fraisch, and the dibble" (505.33) matches the sexual frankness of the Great Litany, as the words represent, respectively, "cuckold," "woman and drunkenness" (combined in German), and "penis." The "Upfellbowm" of four lines earlier may reverse Newton's gravity, but its apple tree (in German) causes the human fall into "fornication and the other deadly sins" that the Litany is so direct in enumerating. This vernacular text of schism opens up the interstices that yoke liturgy and lechery together in a licentiousness bred of liberty.

It is not surprising to find further echoes to phrases exclusively from the Book of Common Prayer. With the universal theme of death and rebirth fundamentally part of the thematics of a book about a wake, the text makes as many references to burial as to sex and marriage. In its resolute, democratic way, the *Wake* is as likely to cite from the Eddas as from any Christian source, yet it does make persistent reference to the Anglican prayer book's order for the burial of the dead. (In fact, the text refers as often to that as to the solemnization of marriage; Hart finds sixteen instances.)[38] In particular, two phrases in common parlance but originally from the Anglican service for the burial of the dead recur as motifs: "ashes to ashes, dust to dust" and "in the midst of life we are in death." The phrases are gospel to a realist like Joyce.

Barbara DiBernard notes that this first phrase ("ashes to ashes") is familiar and that Joyce "makes his own transmutations and combinations."[39] She concludes her analysis of a certain passage by noting, "Joyce has opened our minds to the connections between things, has shown us the true power of words by not limiting them to their denotative meanings." Yet, while universal in appeal, the motif of "ashes to ashes, dust to dust," as she notes, "becomes more than the sum total of its appearances. . . . The essence of [the *Wake*] is repetition and transmutation . . . we watch [phrases] transmute and yet remain the same."[40] What is the same about these phrases, however, putting aside their undeniably similar universal themes, is the fact that they originate with the Anglican prayer book, a fact that gives them a highly denotative register. First off, that opening breach admits other religious traditions, so that ashes come to include the Eddas ("Esk to eshes" [588.28]) or the Druids ("fondoak rushes to the ask" [460.24]), as the dominance of Catholic theology is overthrown.

The theme of death and rebirth is aptly conveyed through the parallel with Humpty Dumpty, the nursery rhyme and the liturgy coming together equally: "so cwypty dwypty what a dustydust it razed arboriginally" (314.16). A Welsh Dumpty is both destroyed ("razed") and echoically lifted up ("raised") from his origins in the tree-based fall ("arbor") of his mortal nature, "dustydust." Lost too in the imperial domain is his aboriginal culture. He is, importantly, someone not English, a native who is captured in a phrase from the prayer book of the imperial culture.

The cycle of death and new life is intimately connected to the natural world, so that the famous phrase becomes "dusk to dusk" (158.08) or "douls a doulse" (588.28), pain and seaweed—a gloss, I think, of Synge's *Riders to the Sea*. That the entire echo is "Esk to esches, douls a doulse! Since Allen Rouge loved Arrah Pogue" adds again a suggestion of marriage and kissing with a reference to the Boucicault play that was as widely known in the culture as the phrase from the prayer book.

The motif of ashes is enlarged to include the Lenten service of Ash Wednesday and to embrace a gendered parody of the phrase that appears in both the Catholic vernacular and Anglican services for that day, "remember man that thou art dust." In Joyce's revision, "Remember, maid, thou dust art powder but Cinderella thou must return" (440.26), the change from the liturgy's "man" to Joyce's "maid" equals the change from poor to rich familiar in the both Cinderella fairytale and the pantomime of popular culture, as well as in the transformative changes wrought by cosmetic powder (with a pun in powder on the Latin "pulvis est"). (There is also a distant echo of the grave scene in *Hamlet* where the Prince instructs Horatio to tell his Lady "to paint an inch thick.") In another place where Joyce echoes the liturgical phrase as "Maid of ashes" (436.02), we hear a reverberation of the poem "Maid of Athens," which raises the figure of Byron. It was Byron for whom Stephen suffers his martyrdom at Heron's hands in *Portrait*, in the scene where Stephen is torn by schismatic impulses.

The other very familiar phrase from the burial service is "in the midst of life we are in death." Joyce's variation, "living in the midst of debt" (11.32), connects to the economics Joyce inevitably linked to the Anglican imperialist enterprise and backward from there to the Reformation schism. Joyce was at the very least consistent in his application of the features he saw in Protestant culture represented by the Anglican prayer book. If Protestantism was not logical in its theology, Joyce would make it logical in its thematics.

Although he was familiar with the marriage service in 1905, Joyce became closely aware of the Anglican prayer book while writing the *Wake* in Paris. He owned two copies of the Book of Common Prayer, one in English and one in French. (Certainly Joyce's knowledge of this text in different languages contributed to the *Wake's* open polyphony, as well as to its enactment of schismatic breaks in liturgical context.)[41] We know from Ellmann that while Joyce was in Paris in the thirties, he questioned Arthur Laubenstein, a young American studying at the prestigious college for organists, "about elements in the Episcopal scripture."[42] While this later American source might be helpful, it would introduce complexities of attribution and citation. The American Episcopal prayer book, revised in 1929 from an earlier 1899 version, differed from the unrevised Anglican one that had been in use since 1662. While it contained the same phrases from the order for burial ("ashes to ashes") and from the Great Litany (the intercessory "We beseech thee to hear us", as well as the deprecatory, "the world, the flesh, and the devil") it asked in this last to be delivered "from inordinate and sinful affectations" omitting the rather telling and frank phrase "from fornication and other deadly sins" that Joyce certainly must have relished. Moreover, the American prayer book's solemnization of marriage did not include the crucial and direct "with my body I thee worship, with my worldly goods I thee endow" a phrase whose acknowledgment of sexual and material realities Joyce clearly regarded as the source of Protestantism's attractive liberation from Catholic silence and repression. What Joyce may have gleaned from Laubenstein, therefore, could only have added to his already existing awareness of worship through the Anglican prayer book and its concomitant effect in the daily life of English-speaking culture through common usage of phrases in popular life. That the American and English prayer books would differ would certainly have affirmed for Joyce, when writing the *Wake*, the multiplicity of his approaches; that they differed would contribute very strongly as well to his lifelong inclination to schism and fascination with religions in which there are repeated breaks from monolithic authority. English as a language might dominate the world, but his Anglican worship was hardly unitary and universal.

One more phrase found in both both American and Anglican prayer books—"give peace in our time"—was universalized in Neville Chamberlain's statement on his return from Munich in 1939. (Not too late for the *Wake*, although the three appearances of the phrase in the work are spread over an area elaborated much earlier.) Again, that persistent association for Joyce of license, money, and appetites applies—as a wish for pleasure and generosity in "send treats in their times" (92.22); as a bedtime request in "grant sleep in hour's time" (259.04); and as a wish to end sectarianism broadcast through the power of the daily press in "Christ in our Irish times" (500.13).

This complementary contrarianism continues throughout the *Wake* in references to the Bible itself: to cite from scripture, we noted at the outset of this chapter, is to appeal to the Protestant sense of autonomous authority derived from the individual act of reading—as Cranmer says in his collect, "to read, mark, learn, and inwardly digest" a text. Yet, in the larger view of the *Wake* it would also convey that special aural quality that would include what the Catholic catechist Deharbe enjoins the faithful to do, "hear and listen." Many scriptural echoes in *Finnegans Wake* are from the Bible proper, but phrases common to both the Douay and King James versions again work against the unitary claim of Catholicism. It is crucial to note that in Trieste Joyce owned a copy of the Authorized Version, along with the Vulgate Latin and an Italian translation, but not a Douay.[43] Much as with his use of the Authorized Version in copying Revelation, this possession can be regarded as a declaration of independence from his upbringing and now also a financial commitment on his part: when he chose with his pocketbook to have a Bible to hand, it would be the Anglican one, making his view of the monetary world of England consistent with his choice of scripture. Atherton notes "the translation he used was the Authorized Version; this appears from the wording of the bulk of his quotations."[44] Early in Dublin and late in Paris, Joyce chose the English Bible.

Take as an example—one that connects beginnings with ends—the meaningful opening of the Gospel of John, the author of Revelation: "The word was made flesh and dwelt among us." The phrase is the same in the Douay Bible and Authorized Version. The passage certainly sanctions the work that Joyce sought to do from the beginning of his career making art an act of living creation. The changes wrought on this famous phrase in the *Wake* speak to much of Joyce's creative literary endeavor. "Babes awondering in the wold made fresh" (336.16) is the fairytale of all narrative wonders, in Eden first of all, (and connected to all written history by the phrase that follows, "where the hen in the storyabout we start from scratch"). Language, the artist's medium, is éclatant, itself a revelation to connect to John's other text, "where flash becomes word" (267.16) and language is the source of all movement as meaning: "In the beginning was the gest" (468.05). This latter phrase is particularly rich with the genetics of all of Joyce's work, from his early interest in the theory of language as gesture (from the Abbe Jousse) to his interest in the comedic jest.

That so universally apt a passage might be taken from either the Catholic or Anglican Bible again stresses the true catholicity of Joyce's use of scripture as the text neither of the one church nor the other but as the text of both and therefore neither, even while maintaining a heretical authority by citing from scripture at all. Pursuing the idea of word and flesh in art, Joyce several times echoes a phrase from the Magnificat of Mary in Luke 1: 38, "Behold the handmaid of the Lord." The same in both bibles, this phrase, true to the spirit of the Incarnation, is connected with physicality and mass in the school lesson's "handmade of the load" (278.12) and with erotic attraction to underclothing in "behold our handmades for the lured" (239.10). (To challenge the purity of Catholic Mariolatry is a preoccupation for Joyce. The description of Polly Mooney being "a little perverse madonna" [D 63] works to the same end.) The Bible can be a source of jest when it appealed to Joyce's schismatic tendencies. When it served the erotic, it challenged the silence of the church. However, when Joyce had to choose a version as a source for scriptural echoes in his works—because to choose is the meaning and the method of heresy—he picked the Bible of the other, not the Douay but the Authorized Version. There are passages in the *Wake* that can only be found in the Protestant English Bible, the one Joyce bought. When forced to choose, Joyce, consistent to his heretical impulses, always chose the schismatic.

Perhaps the choice was made in favor of the Protestant English Bible because its "ear" for English speech was surer, (or, more accurately, its original "ear" became the tongue of the growing literary language). In the Authorized Version's Psalm 68:13, there is the interesting phrase describing a fallen state remedied by divine help: "though ye have lien among the pots, ye shall be as the wings of the dove." In the Douay the line is less immediately comprehensible as "If you sleep among the midst of lots" (67:14). (The line is obviously ambiguous in Hebrew; Tyndale, whose translations make up the Psalter in the Book of Common Prayer, reads it as "though ye have lain among the sheepfold.") With the somewhat clearer idea of pots, Joyce can play with the suggestiveness of the word in the King James Version so that his line in the *Wake* reads, "Though you have lien amung your posspots" (258.16). A drunkard or "tosspot" (a very Jacobean term, hence its appeal to an "ear" like Joyce's attuned to Jonson) and a urinator or "pisspot" mingle in unsavory combination in the *Wake*'s *olla podrida* of a stewpot. (There may also be an echo of "passport" as a reminder of another conundrum: in his exile, Joyce kept his English passport rather than obtain one from the Irish Free State, adhering to English rather than Irish bureaucracy.) The "posspot" also echoes a phrase from one of Joyce's more comical pastiches on a psalm: "Moab is my washpot; over Edom will I cast my shoe" (the Douay has "Moab is my pot of hope; I will stretch out my shoe over Edom"). The phrase appears twice in Psalm 60 and Psalm 108 (Douay 59, 106). The *Wake* sentence goes on from the "posspot" to claim "my excellency is over Ismael" (218.17)—elevating that figure of the outcast, that outsider from the faith, the apostate Joyce saw himself as. Joyce can be ecumenical, embracing all traditions, including the Hebrew, as the passage also contains a parallel with the Jewish Sch'ma: "Thy laud is only as my loud is one." This line combines praise and noise in tribute to the one God, with a sideways glance at the Anglican Bishop Laud (who was horribly burned as Bruno was, but as a martyr to Protestantism). It is in this passage that the phrase "Loud hear us" echoes the Litany so noisily.

Joyce's experience of the Anglican Bible was predicated on intimate reading and on its direct appeal to the reader's conscience and authority (which is why he was drawn to read it as a schismatic), so that he seems to find congenial its tendency to direct address. The parable of the "Ondt and the Gracehoper" has its source not only in Aesop but also in Proverbs. The King James Version addresses the line, "Go to the ant, thou sluggard" (Proverbs 6: 6), directly to the reader in the second person. By contrast, the Douay has a more general, proscriptive vocative, "Go to the ant, o sluggard." Joyce clearly prefers the mode of direct address as befitting the *Wake*'s aural appeal to its audience, an address he maintains in his variation on the Protestant appeal to the hardworking individual: "Thou slogghard" (415.31). One page later, Joyce's freezing Gracehoper reflects on the difference between his and the ant's state by using pronouns of like familiarity: "Me blizzered, him sluggered" (416.21).

The implied intimacy of the King James translators seems to be of a piece with the sexual frankness Joyce saw in the Anglican prayer book. Proverbs contains the quite widely known phrase, "the way of a man with a maid." The Catholic Bible, not surprisingly and in keeping with Joyce's unshakeable sense of the Catholic Church's prudery and silence about sex, gives the line as "a way of a man in his youth." That the phrase from the Anglican source became the title of a pornographic book (to which Bloom alludes in "Sirens" [11.1192]) confirms Joyce's perception of the frankness that accompanied the schismatic turn of Protestantism. Joyce uses the Protestant Bible's line to state a plain maxim of sexual desire even more frankly: "all the way of a man with a maid" (200.26). Here he combines whatever exists in the common awareness of the scriptural line with the slang phrase for sexual conquest, "going all the way."

Joyce similarly, and heretically, chose to echo in the *Wake* the Protestant Bible's Song of Songs (where unabashed eroticism attenuates into allegory). Showing woman as church come to the river's edge in "The Mookse and the Gripes" section, Joyce echoes the familiar phrase, "I am black but comely" (in the Douay, "I am black but beautiful"), as "they say that she was comely" (158.33). To complete the Anglican translation, a few lines earlier the narrator says of her, "I believe she was Black." Later, Joyce varies the Song of Songs line with reference to a woman's hair, "brown but combly" (550.20) This line may well refer to Nora's rich auburn hair or echo Jacob's factory girl who taunts Stephen in *Portrait*: "Do you like what you seen of me, straight hair and curly eyebrows?" (*P* 220). In *Portrait*, Stephen is exposed to the Vulgate Canticum Canticorum Salmonis in the phrase "inter ubera mea commorabitur" (where the overt sexuality of "he shall lie between my breasts" is obscured by the Latin and then allegorized by church exegesis). Given this allusion, surely Stephen knew that the Latin for the phrase "I am black but beautiful" (as the Douay more accurately has it) is "nigra sum, sed formosa." His exposure to the Canticle in *Portrait* occurs through the old prayer book of Alphonse Liguri, so that the Catholic tradition of mediated readings is sustained there in contrast to Joyce's own direct awareness of the Protestant Bible.

One more example of Joyce's use of the Authorized Version in the *Wake* will suffice, and with that example we bring the end of Joyce's scriptural allusions back to its beginning. We noted earlier in this chapter that twice in his early essays Joyce used the Anglican version of the line from Psalm 137, "let my right hand lose its cunning" (the Douay has the unpoetic "Let my right hand be forgotten"). The two citations appear in essays about Ibsen and Dickens, two users of poetic language, the last a prime example of an English author. Of course, the phrase had passed into popular usage and was accessible to Joyce at any turn, but his use of other verses from the Protestant Psalter in the *Wake* speaks quite convincingly to his knowledge of the psalm as a full text, not just as a remembered cultural tag phrase. The psalm opens with "By the waters of Babylon we sat down and wept" (the Douay has "Upon the rivers of Babylon"). The theme of rivers is so central to the *Wake* that ALP's section ends with what is surely an intended parallel, "by the rivering waters of" (216.04). In the Anglican version of the psalm, line two is given as "we hanged our harps upon the willows in the midst thereof." In the Douay, the line appears as "On the willows in the midst thereof we hung up our instruments." For his Wakean echo, Joyce chose the line from the schismatic text, both because the choice itself was heretical and because the Anglican version is more poetic: "where we have hanged our hearts in her trees . . . , by the waters of babalong" (103.10).

This psalm seems particularly resonant as a complaint of exiles, the sorry tale of those who must sing in a foreign land: "For they that carried us away captive required of us a song" (136:3). It is striking that the Authorized Version—as the Bible of the imperial conqueror—uses the word "captive" (the Douay omits it). Joyce's use of the English Bible would indeed appear to enact a dynamic where the language of the conqueror is used by the captive. (This language, as Stephen thinks while talking to the dean of studies, the English convert to Catholicism, was the dean's long before it was the language of Irish writers.) Joyce uses that language, much as he kept his English passport, as a nod to and an appropriation of the conqueror's iconoclasm.

Joyce's use of the Anglican prayer book and the Authorized Version was heretical not only from a sectarian and religious standpoint, but from the standpoint of his native culture's resurgent nationalism. Yet the references in the *Wake* to the Anglican Bible and the Book of Common Prayer come very late in the game. The allusions and echoes in Joyce's early essays and in *Hero* are important parts of Joyce's personal and necessary rebellion against the culture of Catholic Ireland in the beginning of the century. But after Joyce left Ireland for the Continent in 1904 and especially after the establishment of the Free State in 1921, his individual, literary fight against the Roman Catholic Church Universal was greatly attenuated and distanced. Why continue a struggle that was finished long ago?

There remains a reason for Joyce's continued schismatic use of Protestantism to challenge his Irish church and culture, even in a state no longer colonized but free. What Ireland became as an independent country and what position it adopted toward the church, were issues of identity as complex as those raised by its subaltern condition. On these questions of a new Irish identity Joyce would be disappointed, as the independent country asserted a monolithic Gaelic identity and reaffirmed its alignment with church dogma. Severed from Ireland—not as a captive but as an exile—Joyce noted this narrow Gaelic nationalism and accompanying Catholic dogmatism, and they motivated his continued campaign against them through recourse to schismatic Protestant and English texts.

Joyce's use of Protestant texts early in his writing career and later after voluntary exile is driven, then, not only by his need for personal freedom, but by his desire to identify a new direction for independent Ireland. As is so often the case for Joyce, his schismatic turn was a personal choice made in concert with larger issues of art and nation. Joyce's use of schismatic texts serves his early campaign to seize his own freedom and his later efforts to liberate Irish national consciousness from its defining provincialism.

Joyce's early allusion to Anglican texts in a Catholic culture early is related to a challenge facing all Irish writers of the turn of the century: Anglicization. To choose between writing in English or Gaelic was to replay the tension between a dominant power and a rebel camp. The conflict between nationalist and cosmopolitan views of an emerging Irish national identity is the same as the tension between imposed order and openness, between stricture and rebellion from it. Additionally, the question of Anglicization was complicated by the complicity of the Gaelic movement with the Catholic Church. Every Irish writer has had a choice to write either in Gaelic or in English, and Joyce inevitably viewed choice, in religious terms, as heresy.[45]

To go against nationalist conformity with its thoughtless promotion of all things Irish was necessary, Joyce saw, for the integrity of the arts and for the good of the nation and himself. Moreover, he knew that this necessary rebellion would be regarded as apostasy. In a letter to Stanislaus about the Abbey Riots that took place after he left Ireland, Joyce was keenly aware that Synge's choice of language and subject inevitably would be condemned in religious and not aesthetic terms: "Synge will probably be condemned from the pulpit as a heretic." Joyce also recognized that others would be thrilled by the upheaval: AE is "in an excited frame of mind at the amount of heresy that is rife in Dublin" (*Letters* 2:208, 209).

Joyce does not use the term "heresy" merely as a metaphor. He understands that to challenge the nationalist ideal is to challenge the magisterium. For Joyce, the church and the Gaelic movement were so closely allied and complicit that one did the work of the other in precluding any choice for the artist. As early as *Hero*, Stephen wryly notes that the church encourages the faithful to fret over the language question so as to distract them away from unbelief. Yet the opportunity to speak a language different from the conqueror's, Joyce has Stephen say, is an illusory freedom, one of appearance only: "the liberty which they desired for themselves was mainly a liberty of costume and vocabulary" (*SH* 61). For Joyce, true individual and artistic liberty could be obtained only by breaking with strictures imposed by church and nation through acts of heresy. In *Hero*, Stephen uses the term "libery" to describe his resistance to the church: "Jesus or the Church—it's all the same to me. I can't follow him. I must have the liberty to do as I please" (*SH* 140). Joyce well knew that to shrug church authority and authenticate an Irish self meant to seize that liberty which, for him, had fundamentally English roots; his liberation from Catholic authority in his early years had to be schismatic in order for it to be less Irish.

We have noted that Joyce's openness to license, to the material world, and to sexual frankness—all the freedoms that enraged the pious Abbey audience to riot—enabled him to break with his culture and speak of "real life" in his early years as a writer. After 1909, Joyce had to reassert and extend his schismatic authority to challenge the chauvinism of the new Ireland. What had pertained to Joyce's personal life had now extended to that of the new nation.

The Irish Free State in 1922 may have succeeded in defining itself as a nation independent of Britain, but it did so by embracing Rome. This was the exchange that Joyce felt would not succeed: to substitute "English tyranny while the Roman tyranny occupies the palace of the soul" (*CW*, "Saints and Sages" 173). The Free State's "ostentatious commitment to the norms of Catholic social teaching" made it little more than a continued servant of Rome: "in education, as in social law, the state followed the Catholic line[—]divorce was excluded, birth control outlawed."[46] For Joyce, then, the Ireland of 1922 and beyond was still in thrall to a power that required a schismatic challenge.

Joyce turned again to the English Bible—this time to challenge Irish nationalism. It cannot be said for certain whether biblical echoes in the *Wake* are variations on specific quotations or recollections of fragments from a larger, cultural text. But it is from this very uncertainty—in the open space made by schism—that his late purpose for using the Anglican Bible obtains. His method is the same, as are his apostatic and rebellious purposes. Whereas Joyce used the Anglican Bible early in his writing to break free *within* Ireland, by the 1930s he would use it to free Ireland from itself and into a larger world. As a cultural artifact and international resource available for use by any native population in the Empire, the English Bible had enormous value as a tool for communication.[47] In the same passage in *Hero* where Stephen darkly predicts that the church will triumph in Ireland by its assistance to the language movement, he also makes a claim for the power of the English language. When his interlocutor Madden states, "But really our peasant has nothing to gain from English Literature," Stephen responds, "English is the medium for the Continent" (54). Just as Joyce was confirmed in his prediction that the Irish Free State would reempower the Catholic Church, he was equally confirmed in his predictions about the global reach and power of the English language.

By citing the English Bible and the Book of Common Prayer in *Finnegans Wake* (whose title of an Irish-American ballad reaches out to Ireland outremer), Joyce marshals his schismatic tactics and designs to open Ireland to international cultural influences beyond the purview of the Catholic Church. Joyce seeks to induct Ireland into a polyglot world and to universalize it away from its "split little pea" or "p" of "parochialism." In turn, by universalizing Ireland and by promoting English against liturgical use of Latin, Joyce challenges the Catholic Church's claim to universal authority. Joyce would surely have felt vindicated to know that, following World War II, British culture, with the strong support of its American cousin, dominated the world, even if he welcomed only the diminished power of Rome.

Joyce never wholly maintained his turns against or toward religions or ideologies or languages. It was his nature and power as an individual and artist to break through anything that started to ossify or ensnare. He would continue to find ways to challenge church and state hegemony by asserting the power of schismatic acts to rupture, reanimate, and reverse institutional, social, and cultural movements in their own drives to dominate.

# Schism as Politics

Along with the artistic possibilities of schism for Joyce, there could be dividends in the sphere of political action. Through schism, Joyce could resist certain powers in a way that provided freedom of choice in contexts other than the production of art. Eschewing loyalty to the church of his youth and resisting the claims of a nationalism allied with it, he also had no wish to enlist wholeheartedly in the ranks of Britain's global empire. True to his rebellious nature, he would turn against supporting such secular, political powers as Britain. While his alignment with English culture through the Authorized Version and the Anglican prayer book had its uses, it also had its limits. He wanted to be Irish, but Irish free from Britain and Rome and all petty sectarianism. In order to continue resisting the hegemony of the church and its claims to universal power, he sought out schismatic gestures and events that could be regarded as local and native expressions. This kind of resistance would be achieved by Joyce's seeing rents and tears in church history as opportunities for making choices that involved action and national identity. He would use his misbelief to assert a brand of national identity that would be a model for the Ireland he sought to express through his apostasy.

In "Scylla" Stephen names three very unlikely associated figures who have mocked a strongly held point of orthodoxy—the notion of divine relation or "the son consubstantial with the Father": "Photius, pseudo Malachi, Johann Most" (9.492). Stephen emphasizes the figures here, rather than the ideas they represent. They form an enigmatic Trinity containing in its persons a religious figure, a nonce figure apparently religious (and referring to the character Mulligan), and a secular, political figure. Photius we will consider more closely below. As far as Mulligan is concerned, Joyce knew that mockery could be heresy, as demonstrated by Mulligan's parodic Mass in "Telemachus" and the imagined Black Mass in "Circe." Yet not all heresy is made by mockery. There was for Joyce considerably more at stake in heresy than easy humor: there was freedom, artistic choice, and serious political ends. In his discussion of Johann Most, the one figure in the triad who is political rather than literary or religious, Manganiello describes an anarchist "who attacked the Church and the notion of God" in a written parody of the Apostle's Creed. Joyce echoed this parody in "Cyclops": "they believe in rod, the scourger almighty, creator of hell on earth, and in Jacky Tar, the son of a gun" (12.1354).[1] This parody, itself a "ripping good joke," takes a statement of belief and aligns it ironically with the powers of the state, especially the naval power of the British Empire, in a combination that prefigures the possibilities of schism. More seriously, Johann Most wrote *The Science of Revolutionary Warfare* (and was a model for the anarchist Hoffendahl in Henry James' political novel, *The Princess Cassamassima*). Manganiello contends that Stephen's insertion of Most into this discussion constitutes an attack on a society in which evangelists are more important than politicians, where religion leads people away from an engagement with politics.[2] For Manganiello, religion somehow inadequately supersedes politics, and he can only read Stephen's rebellious *non serviam* as a form of anarchy, arguing that the religious rebellion is a metaphor for political reformism. Yet Most's eclectic combination of an attack against the Godhead, a parody of the Trinity, and a manual for revolution may not be so odd or disparate for Joyce: they may be connected in his mind as an example of the usefulness of schism.

Questions regarding the figures of the Trinity to which Stephen alludes appear throughout Joyce's works: the procession of the Holy Ghost in Eastern Orthodoxy in the *Wake*; Stephen's reflections on the Son and the Father—on what is called divine filiation—in *Ulysses*. These Trinitarian issues are all, at one level, pure and simple, questions of relationships of power and equality.[3] Trinitarian challenges appear throughout church history because their questions all concern essential identities and consequently issues of power, equality, and subordination. When Stephen is obsessively concerned with questions of the Son "consubstantial" with the Father, starting in "Proteus" (3.50), he is thinking of his own strained relations with his family and more; he refers to the Nicene Creed which establishes the dogma of the Trinity. It is also true that any debate about the relationship of father to son—of Jesus to His Heavenly Father; of Hamlet and his father, the King; of any son to any father—interrogates power relations. Such debate represents a political battle against patriarchy and the gendered law and enacts the conflict between dominion and subservience. The Joyce concerned with artistic autonomy and independent thought found these questions crucial. For him, religious choice itself could be a form of political action and reaction: issues of dogma and doctrine, what is believed and taught are themselves strictures, like law and economics, that must be confronted and challenged. Most pertinent, the church as an institution of great power and influence resembles the state; it is also a material power in the world. The recurring connection of the church with political and social power was a theme well rehearsed in Joyce's life, starting in his young years. In the threat of the eagle retributively plucking out the eyes of rebellious children in *Portrait* and the pri-

mal scene of Parnell's case—rehearsed at Christmas, no less—we find a conflation of politics and religion. The angry exchange between Dante Riordan, who
supports the priests, and Simon Dedalus, who supports the politicians, makes
an irrevocable rip in the fabric of the family (*P* 32).

Rome touched many of the issues of daily life to which Joyce was committed.
The church obviously enjoined a strict morality through the silence on sexual
matters that Joyce found so repressive of art and liberty. Pope Leo XIII, who
reigned during much of Joyce's youth up to his departure for the Continent,
promulgated several policies that impinged on social and cultural life. For one,
he reinvigorated the sixteenth-century *Index Librorum Prohibitorum* (List of
Prohibited Books) in his 1903 *Index Leonianus*. While the threat of censure was
greater than the actual repression, the chilling effect upon artistic expression
was unmistakable.[4] Leo also took a stand on economic issues, issuing a papal
bull against Socialism in *De Rerum Novarum* (1886) to counteract its universal appeal to the working class.[5] In particular, in its ultramontane tendencies
against what it called "Modernism"—defined by the *Catholic Encyclopedia* as
"a spirit of complete emancipation, tending to weaken ecclesiastical authority"
(10:416)—the church stood firmly for a conservative reluctance to embrace new
ideas and tendencies.[6] Foremost among these tendencies was the claim that
"the law of the Church does not extend to . . . the practice of scholarly exegesis."[7] For Joyce, who used liturgical texts for his own interpretive and creative
purposes, this charge struck close to home. That the president of University
College as depicted in *Hero* could mistakenly (and easily) elide Modernism, as
an issue of ethics and authority, with the modern trend in art as exemplified by
Ibsen and Zola only confirmed Joyce's sense of the pervasive and uninformed
intrusion of the church into the disparate contexts of life and art.

Joyce engages religion as a battle of ideas in the lived world of history; this
is a battle he saw looming and worth fighting over, even in the most arcane
religious questions that seemed remote from everyday life.[8] The intellectual
imagination he trumpets through the character of Stephen Dedalus represents
an ideational challenge beyond doctrine. If the struggle, for Joyce, was waged
first for the high stakes of art, it would also be waged for social action.

Thus Joyce views any religious controversy as a political confrontation; religious choice (the meaning of heresy) becomes political action against the
status quo. The exercise of religion, especially in defiance, is the exercise of
political will through the creation of an individual identity in contrast to an
institutional one. Schism and heresy can be seen as local movements, narrow
rebellions against centralized hegemony. To regard Joyce's interest in religious
challenge as a parallel to his artistic independence is to move from mere anticlericalism to a different sort of nationalism—one separate from the Gaelic

League and predicated on disobedience to Rome in order to assert localized identity.[9] To fight the powers of church and state required human models of rebellion—models who, while attacking church theology, made clear that political change would emerge from the challenge. Much as Joyce's art benefited from his schismatic turn, the rebellion of certain historical heretics offered him opportunities in the political sphere.

The passage from "Scylla," cited at the head of this chapter, provides an opportunity to meet such heretics; there, along with the political figure Most, Stephen also names Photius, the one religious figure. In this naming Joyce returns to the exotic East where he began his art of epiclesis. From the orthodox Catholic point of view, Photius was a schismatic of the first water, responsible for the original split in the Church Universal, a split that had both theological and practical consequences. By the child emperor, Michael III, under the guidance of his uncle the regent, Photius was named bishop or patriarch of Constantinople over his predecessor Ignatius. Ignatius objected to the morals of the regent Bandas, and his claim to the See was favored by Pope Nicholas I in Rome. Photius' appointment was thus marked by political divisions. Photius was excommunicated by the Pope with the support of a Synod of the Lateran in 863. In a turn that Joyce certainly would have favored, Photius himself excommunicated the Pope and the Latins; his charges against them, among other things, were that they forbade priestly marriages and that they added the filioque clause to the Nicene Creed. When we remember that the Eastern Church engaged the epiclesis that characterized Joyce's early writing and that the filioque clause resurfaces in the *Wake*, we see that Joyce's evocation of and Stephen's appeal to Photius are consistent with the Joyce canon.

What Stephen evokes in "Scylla"—in reference to Photius and his position on the persons of the Trinity—is the schismatic as a historical figure who challenges power.[10] Photius represents a clear example of someone who makes a drastic change in the structure of power by choosing religious defiance as a course of action. What begins as a doctrinal challenge serves a political one.[11] As bishop of Constantinople, Photius challenged Rome in the matter of the Trinity; by asserting that the Holy Ghost does not proceed from the Father and the Son, Photius indirectly challenged all relations of personhood in the three spheres of the Trinity as unequal distributions of authority. Stephen's reference to Photius may also be read with regard to the heretic's ideas about the material allocation of state power. Photius was instrumental in defying the central authority of the bishopric of Rome, challenging Rome's increasing subordination of Constantinople's authority in the matter of the clerical administration of a diocese in Greece. This was a power struggle pure and simple. Both of these stances, the theological and the political (and of course they are connected), led to the eventual establishment of the Eastern Church and the Great Schism in the Church Universal. Photius' individual action, exemplifying the rending or disruption of religious hegemony, is what Joyce sought in the spaces of schism. Stephen's naming Photius along with the political Johann Most speaks to two aspects of the political dimension of religion: first, marginal resistance to dogma as an imposition of power (dogma in Photius' case involved the distribution of power in the Trinity); and second, individual resistance to the actual authorized power of an institution that claims universality.

As discussed in chapter 1, heresy appears in *Portrait* only as adolescent rebellion against a school authority backed by the church. In this early context, heresy functions in Joyce's writing as route to artistic possibilities. In *Ulysses*, the heresy theme is broadened to include actual schism against real powers at work in the historical world. Where in *Portrait* Stephen playacts as a heretic in parodying the rector, others have been actual heretics to serious ends; where schism makes art possible, it also makes action feasible. Schism for Joyce has a noble pedigree. Heresy is the ultimate exercise of the political freedom of choice, the fundamental political act against any established structure, religious or civil. As heresies seek to overturn the dominant power structures of the status quo, they are, by extension, revolutionary. Heresy is an assertion of individual will, creating agency and identity both by choice and by the definition of the self in contrast to the dominant power. It is the same freedom of action in political choice that Joyce sought for himself in artistic choice.[12]

Joyce configures religion as politics in the context of two ultimate sources of enfranchisement and power. First are those questions of the Trinity, whose related affiliations and powers have often been the source of rents in the historical identity of divine authority. Second, by sequent extension, Joyce configures religion as politics by interrogating the power of the church as an institution (representing that divine power), whose authority in deciding such matters he must resist. The two issues are completely related and not merely analogs: filiation is transmitted power (with the implication of subservience and subalternity), and the church that asserts the filiation through dogma maintains its institutional power. (This is why Johann Most, the anarchist, would attack the state through revolution and the evangelical church and the notion of the Godhead through mockery.) Joyce is persistently interested in that seemingly wholly theological problem of the nature of the Trinity—those schisms like the filioque controversy, Arianism, and Sabellianism, that in different ways challenge the orthodoxy of the body of God—because that body, by extension, is the body politic. The Nicene Creed figures in *Ulysses* because Stephen resists the connections it implies about his personal identity as a son within a family; it appears in the "Proteus" section where he thinks of himself as a son "made not begotten" (3.45) in contrast to the Son, in the words of the Creed, as "begotten, not made." As regards the identity of the state, however, the Creed figures for Joyce as a statement about an authority that sought to squelch local, national identities. Raised a Catholic, Joyce is particularly interested in assaulting the unitary power of the Vatican, both in religious terms and in terms of hegemony; being Irish, he is particularly resistant to the subsuming of his local identity as a Dubliner into the larger one of a universal Catholic. All the challenges he poses to the established power of the church are revolutionary because they seek to diminish a dominant power; they are revolutionary as well, because they are local and native in the service of a marginalized and peripheral identity.

For this reason, heretics as particular persons and agents appear as almost obsessive components in Stephen's thinking and are widely present in Joyce's work. For Joyce, heretics present crucial issues of individual choice and, consequently, of identity in the same terms as do theological questions about the Trinity. We can sense the urgency of these issues for Joyce and Stephen in the ways that heretics appear in contexts that are otherwise not about religion but about secular power and politics in history. One signal connection appears in the first chapter of *Ulysses*, in the "Telemachus" discussion about history's being to blame for Irish subservience. In seeking to accuse "history," Haines asks Stephen whether he is not his own master; through that question Haines assumes a Byronic or Nietzschean stance. Stephen begins his discussion of his political powerlessness engendered by history by observing that he is the servant of three masters—England, Italy (or Rome), and Ireland (or Irish Catholicism)—in terms of their declining relative powers. Stephen therefore appears to answer Haines' political query with the Marxist notion of the master/slave dialectic, but his thoughts turn quickly from philosophy or economics to religion proper. He follows his train of thought not by reciting a mental litany of expected Irish political moments and grievances (a list that Haines and the reader might reasonably expect), but rather by naming the church itself as an entity, which has undergone, Stephen thinks, a slow growth and change of dogma.

> The proud potent titles clanged over Stephen's memory the triumph of their slow brazen bells: *et unam sanctam et apostolicam ecclesiam*: the slow growth and change of rite and dogma like his own rare thoughts. . . . Symbols of the apostles in the mass for pope Marcellus, their voices blended. (1.650–54)

First, Stephen acknowledges, while he seeks to resist, the historically unitary power of the "one holy and apostolic" church in the Latin of the Nicene Creed.

This is certainly a historical perspective, but its organicist model of the church, if Stephen compares it to his own mind's growth and change, does not suggest a flexibility of the church spiritual to challenges. While Rome may have adopted the harmonic church music of Palestrina (which may seem to Stephen to be its only modern concession), it is on guard against schism: behind the music, Stephen thinks, stands the church militant—for Stephen, surely the ultimate power.

> The vigilant angel of the church militant disarmed and menaced her heresiarchs. A horde of heresies fleeing with mitres awry: Photius, and the brood of mockers whom Mulligan was one, and Arius, warring his life long upon the consubstantiality of the Son with the Father, and Valentine, spurning Christ's terrene body, and the subtle African heresiarch Sabellius who held that the Father was Himself His own Son. (1.655–60)

In addition to the trio of Photius, PseudoMalachi, and Most, Joyce has Stephen enlarge the pantheon of apostasy: Mulligan is still here, and Photius has pride of place, but Arius, Valentine, and Sabellius are added. (The first of these two by their heresies, the last by his locality.) The names of individual heretics are singled out to stand each one against the corporate entity of the church. By removing the Latin phrase "unam sanctam catholicam et apostolicam ecclesiam" from its historical context, Stephen identifies the church as just such an entity, thereby foregrounding its institutionalism and impersonality as something with effective, actual power in the world—the church as a force. The church's status as a material establishment, its institutionalism, is also easily confused with the spirituality inherent to the doctrinal Institution of the Eucharistic sacrifice by Christ at the Last Supper that forms the basis of the church's legitimacy among believers. Like the unnamed boy in "The Sisters" who thinks of "how complex and mysterious were certain institutions of the Church" [*D* 13], Stephen elides the two concepts—the Eucharist and the establishment—when he thinks about the church's power and effect.

The "unam sanctam catholicam et apostolicam ecclesiam" for Stephen is the main point: the unity of the church is the source of its claim to universal power, and to challenge that unity, through various gestures of schism, is to undermine that force. The source of the phrase Stephen cites is most apt, because it comes from the Nicene Creed, the statement of orthodox faith whose intent was not only to affirm belief but to suppress dissent in the universal body of the church regarding the nature of the Trinity. All theological questions of the Son's being (the hypostasis), his relation with the Father, and the procession of the Holy Ghost were decided by the dogmatic statement of the First Nicene

Council of 325. Pertinent to the issue of individual holders of heterodox positions, that council particularly stated that there are "those who say: There was a time when He was not, and He was not before He was begotten; and that He was made out of nothing; or who maintain that He is of another hypostasis or another substance, or that the Holy Ghost is created, or mutable, or subject to change," and "[them] the Catholic Church anathematizes" (*CE*, "Councils of Nicea" 11:45). The Council of Nicea's statement of dogma on the theological positions was encoded in the Creed of 381. The individuals whom Stephen names have been excluded by the assertions of the Creed, cast out as heretics and erased.

While it was because of their theological positions on the nature of the Son and His relationship with the Father that these figures were ostracized as heretics, it is their historical identities as real persons that matters most to Stephen who focuses as much on the actors as on their ideas. Their heresies for Joyce meant literally their choices, but his connection to them goes deeper than etymology. The heretics chose to persist in and practice their ideas, even after those ideas had been judged erroneous (much as Joyce emulated, by willingly holding to, the heretical side of the already-decided controversies). Those choices, moreover, involved not only the taking of a stance *for* a religious belief but also *against* a dominant power (for Joyce, a highly desirable action). To deny the divinity of the Son or to deny His being one with the Father is to undermine delegated and delineated structures of authority. Thus it is that Stephen names Photius (for the second time in *Ulysses*) and includes Sabellius and Arius as leaders of heresies who each sought to defy the power of the church orthodoxy by redefining the body of the Godhead. By so doing and thus defying the church's political hegemony, its dominion over the state, they acted as free persons, thereby resisting the extremely effective institution of the church's dominion over their lesser entities. Inevitably, as challengers of the church's secular arm, the heretics and their theological ideas were suppressed in the dogma asserted by the Nicene Creed. The Creed tried to erase Arius and Sabellius by not naming them or their controversial ideas as Arian or Sabellian heresies. By contrast, Stephen restores their individuality by naming them. Moreover, Stephen maintains their particular existence (as we shall see a little further on) by reviving their names and their local and native identities.

Photius makes his appearance the first time in *Ulysses* in the earlier-cited passage from "Telemachus," but he is always already for Joyce marked as the originator of the schism of the Eastern Church. Of the other heresiarchs Stephen mentions—Sabellius, Arius, and, less crucially, Valentine—he stresses their political identities and implied histories as much as their heterodox opinions. Sabellius, for one, is given a local identity. The ideas matter less than who promulgated them and where those individuals came from. Stephen names them to emphasize the details of their lives, which otherwise would have been erased by authoritative power.

First chronologically—although mentioned last by Stephen—Sabellius (flourished AD 217–20) is a Monarchian who denied that the Godhead was anything other than a monad in three operations; he thus denied any filiation. If it was not so initially, this position became heretical. Sabellius is said in the *Catholic Encyclopedia* to have been "a leader of the Monarchians in Rome," undermining that increasing center of power. The *Encyclopedia* also notes, highlighting that alien or exotic quality attractive to Joyce, that "Sabellianism is an Eastern term for the Monarchian modalists" (10:449). Arius is the most intriguing case. In the fourth century, Arius accused his own bishop of Sabellianism—a charge certainly rooted in power struggle, treachery, and betrayal. Arius himself believed that God is unique but that, unlike the Father, the Son is a wholly created being. For this he was challenged in his turn by his superior, Peter, Bishop of Alexandria. Joyce was always fascinated by charge and countercharge and the grievances that power causes in its own execution. The idea that the Son is a wholly created being Stephen takes to heart in "Proteus." When he thinks of his own relationship to his "consubstantial" father and of his own existence as "made, not begotten," he has occasion to think of Arius for the second time (3.50–52). Stephen willingly connects himself to the heretic, because he wishes to deny his own filial and subordinated relations. Arius, according to the *Catholic Encyclopedia*, is said to have been part of "the Eastern attempt to rationalize [the Son's identity] by stripping [the] mystery . . . of the relation of Christ to God"—an act of unveiling and ripping that certainly would appeal to the Stephen who, on Sandymount, shuts his eyes to see (*CE*, "Arianism" 1:707). Both Arius and his thinking were condemned as heretical by the Council of Nicea, which established as dogma in the Creed that the Son is "of one being with the Father, begotten not made." Arius' claims against the consubstantiality of the Son were a reformulation of the older Gnostic heresy, which projected a knowable "conjugation" of divine power and a deep, unknowable God. So that here, *mutatis mutandis*, recurs the suspicion of the East in the oldest of heresies, the Gnostic, of which Valentine was a foremost proponent. (Stephen listing him between Arius and Sabellius is logically consistent.) Gnosticism was a heresy from the earliest days of the church, and it may figure, we noted, in the earliest of Joyce's stories, "The Sisters."

Not only by a sort of religious credence does the orthodox definition of the Trinity express powers; the church that defines these powers becomes a potent agent, monolithic and centralized. The power of the church against these heresiarchs and their heresies particularly fascinates Joyce: the persecuted heresiarchs are avatars of the Joycean conviction of always-possible betrayal and paranoia, as Arius' curious history of accusing turn and counterturn illustrates. (Newman appealed to Stephen along a similar trajectory of conversion and challenge.) Stephen's citing of terms from the Nicene Creed on the unity and continuity of the church is pertinent to the struggle for political power. The Creed is not only the statement of dogma against which the willful choice of heresy is defined; it becomes the expression of the stated power of the central authority (effectively Rome) that suppresses the local periphery. Pertinently, and in particular, these heresies take place where religious orthodoxy bullied actual political states and persons, where local religious interpretations were suppressed by central authority.

Stephen and Joyce see that the Creed erases not only interpretations of the Trinity that are multiple and diverse, but local, even native, traditions as well. Stephen recognizes in his citation that the Council of Nicea's purpose was to unify and centralize dogma–the right thinking of hegemony—but he also realizes that its effect was to squelch multiple interpretations and individual, marginal expressions. That these expressions—and the individuals who voiced them—are invariably seen as local and marginal is precisely the point. That is why the figures Stephen names are individualized beyond their positions as heretics by their local identities. Their heresies assert just such native identity. When he discusses the actors in these heretical ruptures, Stephen localizes them by associating them with a particular place or event: Sabellius is an African bishop (1.659); Arius dies in a Greek watercloset (3.52). The reach of the dominant power in distant Rome is long, extending to far-away lands and territories. No one in Ireland could fail to feel the political parallel.

It is just this sense of nativism that motivates Stephen in "Telemachus" to call Sabellius "a subtle African heresiarch" and, again in "Scylla," "the African" (9.862)—Africa being a colony on the margin of power. He similarly estranges Arius in "Proteus" by describing his death in a "Greek watercloset," where "Greek" is understood to mean alien. The marginalization of the alien is borne out by what little is known of Arius, even in the dogmatic but comprehensive text of the *Catholic Encyclopedia*. He is "said to be a Libyan by descent," a certainly vague enough geographical placement that allows extrapolation ("Arius" 1:718). In the same way, the Gnostics of Valentine were Manicheans of a very localized set in Palestine. Thus in mentioning the Nicene Creed, Stephen acknowledges it as a statement that consolidates power and also as a document that erases and suborns local expressions.

It is to these rebellions as native and local struggles that Joyce is particularly drawn in his depictions: to Photius who embodies the Eastern Church's break from the increasingly centralized authority of Rome; to Arius, whose foreign identity is indicated by his death in a Greek water closet; and to Sabellius, who on scant evidence is nonetheless identified as an African bishop. (Sabellius was a presbyter of Rome; his views were adopted in Libya by Arius; thus, by a sort of local solidarity Stephen claims Sabellius as an African.) Each of the unique identifiers associated with Joyce's (and Stephen's) heretics emphasize their marginality to mainstream religious authority. Stephen foregrounds the heretics' local origins in order to reclaim from the hegemony subordinated native ideas and the individuals who generated them. This is a political morphology pertinent to all movements of liberation: an assertion of the vitality of native tradition (here, religious tradition) taken back from the imperial endeavor. Thus it is that Joyce finds in these heresies not only ideological challenges to ecclesiastical authority, but particularly personal challenges to political authority, local uprisings against a distant centralized power as avatars of all attempts at colonial liberation. Africa, Libya, Roman Palestine all seem to be road signs to a yet-to-be-realized liberation from empire. Ireland must take its place in such a queue.

Joyce's view that heresy is a localized religious form or expression suppressed by a distant central power and thus the embodiment of a nativist, colonized stance is, arguably, his most particular twist on religion as politics. That is why Stephen's consideration of the Britisher Haines' comments about local Irish history turns to thoughts about the church militant against all its heresies rather than to Irish historical events. Joyce sees heresy not simply as a religious rebellion but as the equivalent of nationalism, a way to express an identity.

And if there must be local resistance to the church's unity and authority in history, so too must there be resistance to the unitary and exclusive view of the Irish nationalism that supported Rome in Joyce's time. Throughout his work, Joyce steadfastly yokes religion and politics, a combination frequently evinced in his disgust over the complicity of Irish nationalism with the Roman Church. It is logical, then, that he would seek to assert religious apostasy as a form of nativist political action. The rising and exclusive power of a Gaelic League, backed by the hegemony of Rome, needed to be resisted by something schismatic and local. Crucial to this campaign is Joyce's particular reading of Irish history in the lecture "Saints and Sages." Here he claims that English dominance is less threatening to Ireland than that of Rome, adding that England stopped persecuting the church when the church itself "became an effective instrument of subjugation" (*CW* 166). The overwhelming power of the Roman Church drove Joyce to pursue his own schism by turning to English religious texts as sources for his art in order to resist the Gaelic League's definition of Irish culture. Moreover, in the real world of politics—alongside and consistent with this claim of resistance to the unitary and universal power of the church—Joyce strongly challenged the Gaelic League's misrepresentation of Irish identity as something similarly unitary and absolute. The unity of Catholic dominance in Ireland, Joyce argues, is supported by the assertion of one, true Celtic Race—an assertion made with all the arrogance that informed the church's claims of universal authority. It is this fiction of unity Joyce challenges.

For Joyce, the fiction of a unitary Irish identity is to be challenged by a counterclaim of multiplicity. As Joyce supported challenges to the presumed identity of the Church of Rome in history, so too would he support a challenge to accepted Irish one; single orthodoxy must be met by heterodoxy, homogeneity questioned by heterogeneity. Joyce resists the unitary claim of racial purity, of a bloodline unmixed. He asserts in the Irish makeup "a new Celtic Race," "another national temperament [rose] on the foundation of the old one, with the various elements" of the old Celtic stock "mingling" with "Scandinavian, Anglo-Saxon, and Norman races"(*CW* 161); he thus valorizes a heterodizing mixture of bloodlines. This multiplicity produces "a vast fabric in which the most diverse elements are mingled, in which Nordic aggressiveness and Roman law, the new bourgeois conventions and the remnant of a Syriac religion are reconciled" (*CW* 165). A fabric, as Joyce well knew, could get a rip in it, a schismatic rupture, but certainly a fabric that includes multiple and disparate elements is far less likely to succumb to strain. By the *Wake*, Joyce has transformed his argument of Ireland's ethnic and cultural diversity into art: "Miscegenations on miscegenations" (18.20), where mixed blood makes up a true nation.

If there is no longer a unitary Irish race, there is no easy unity between an Ireland of mixed influences and a church in Rome which, confronted by the local heretical challenges of history, can hardly claim to be universal. And it is in this connection that Joyce claims the power of Ireland in challenging Rome in history, by naming local Irish heretics who, like Photius and Sabellius, were localized in marginal places and challenged the central authority of Rome in their capacities as natives.

In "Ireland, Island of Saints and Sages," Joyce does not give a litany of expected Irish saints, such as Columbanus or Fiacre, any more than Stephen answers Haines on history with a list of Irish grievances. Instead, he claims as its contribution to the European Church of the 6th through 8th centuries that "Ireland has the honour of producing three great heresiarchs: John Duns Scotus, Marcarius, and Vergilius Solvagius" (*CW* 160). He calls them heretics on the basis of their nationalities; he seems to prize their heterodoxy from Rome as some measure of their Irish national identity. In this, his maneuver mirrors Stephen's when, on slight evidence, he establishes the local identities of Sabellius and Arius and envisions heterodoxy as a local achievement. In order to make such connections, Joyce, like Stephen, must also make attenuated claims about those he names. As none were great and none particularly heretical, he has to exaggerate their claims to both apostasy and nationality.[13] It is as if in order to be Irish in Joyce's eyes, one must be a heretic in those of the church. He pursues this tenuous connection (asserting it precisely because of its tenuousness) because he rightly asserts the actual claim of the Roman Church as an instrument of subjection. Moreover, Joyce appears to confuse John Scotus Erigena, not a heretic, with John Duns Scotus, also not a heretic, whatever excesses Scholasticism subsequently committed.[14] The confusion rests entirely on Joyce's focus on "Scotus" as the determining mark, by which toponymic Joyce wishes to claim a Gaelic connection at least as alien as a Scot, with his additional error of thinking that "Duns" makes the figure (darkly) Irish. Actual identity counts for less here than imputed or implied qualities of national character. Joyce plays equally elastically with notions of heresy, seeming to grant to his churchmen a measure of disobedience he wishes to claim as an Irish national trait, much as it was his own personal one.

Vergilius Solvagius was an Irishman, but no heretic. He held that a baptism performed by an ignorant priest with the wrong words was valid and was reported to Pope Zachary by Boniface. In turn—and this must have been what appealed to Joyce—Boniface also charged him with contending that the earth was round contrary to the scriptures, but Vergilius succeeded in defending himself from charges of teaching false doctrine. Marcarius was a minor figure who wrote on Averroës, an action accounted heretical in part because of Averroës' being an alien (Arabian, hence Eastern) figure whose identity as a foreigner was more threatening than that as a thinker.

Joyce extends the badge of apostasy as racial trait even to a figure of disputed nationality. In the same lecture, Joyce makes the logically tenuous claim that "Pelagius, a traveler and a tireless propagandist, if not an Irishman, as many contend, was certainly either Irish or Scottish" (CW 157). Pelagius was in fact a heresiarch, disputed by no less a figure than Augustine for his conviction that mankind was essentially good and free, not inherently sinful and in need of Grace. Pelagius' views are more universal than specifically national (or Irish), so his identity as a Scot or Irishman is questionable. Especially evasive in its construction—"if not an Irishman, [Pelagius] was certainly either Irish or Scottish"—Joyce's claim that Pelagius must be a fellow national seems to issue from his own exercise of free thought. Pelagius' background is sketchy, and his real name, Morgan, is Celtic but not necessarily Irish.

[A brief excursus. While Judaism hardly insists upon the universality or dogmatic conformity that the Roman Church does, Bloom is certainly a heterodox figure. In *Ulysses*' "Circe" episode, he is associated with figures of Jewish apostasy—as they appear in literature, such as the son of Nathan in the play; in Jewish apocrypha, such as "The Messiah Ben Joseph" (15.1843); and in history, such as the directly named Abulafia (15.1907) or as another heretic nominated by place, Laemlein of Istria (15.1907). Bloom's interest in Spinoza may be due less to his philosophy (and the volume inherited from his father) than to the frisson occasioned by Spinoza's ostracism from the Jewish community for heresy. Though Irish, Bloom doesn't fit the standard of Gaelic racial purity; he is neither precisely Catholic nor Protestant (despite being baptized in each faith), and he is not a Jew. He comes from another place, the East (Szombathely, London). His somewhat uncertain origins contribute to his identity as a student of misbelief, a position that makes him worldly and somewhat wise in his resistance and resilience. Joyce was scrupulously fair in assigning the virtue of misbelief to Jews as well as Gentiles.]

Returning to Joyce's claims, on slight grounds of either heresy or nationality of these "Irish" figures in this essay and from the "African" claims about Sabellius and Arius in "Proteus," Joyce asserts that religion is politics and apostate rebellion a form of political nativism. This connection is maintained—as in nearly all of his schismatic turns—throughout his writings: it appears not only in the "Saints and Sages" lecture of 1907 or *Ulysses* in 1922, but at the end in *Finnegans Wake*. The appeal of schism is strong, and Joyce is faithful to it in his way. The questions pursuing the conflict between Shem and Shaun (book 1, chapter 6) are usually regarded as opposites in tension, "polarized forces" such as space and time.[15] Nonetheless, there seems to be throughout the passage a particular quality of conflict as between unequal powers: superior and inferior; centralized and local; narrow and universal—all encapsulated by the greatest disproportion of all, orthodoxy and heresy. In fact, the "Mookse and the Gripes" episode is a reprise of issues that Joyce saw as intrinsically connected: power, rebellion, and religion, each comprised of universal and local pairs. If we have previously treated this section as the last in Joyce's consistent schismatic attraction to the Eastern Church, we must also acknowledge that it is also a section about an apostasy much closer to home, equally schismatic but more local. That the same section of the *Wake* can contain two different issues is further proof—were it needed—that it contains multitudes. Yet more than multiplicity challenges unitary meaning: the Great Schism and local apostasy are clearly combined in Joyce's mind as complements in a dynamics of rending.

At first, the passage involves the conflict between Adrian IV (153.20) or the English "Bragspear" (152.36) and Ireland as a consequence of the bull *Laudibiliter* (154.20)—for Joyce, clearly a matter of the loss of local sovereignty to distant powers conveniently played out in a religious context of obedience and resig-

nation: "I connow make my submission, I cannos give you up" (154.34).[16] The
Mookse, emerged from the vast wealth of his palace and resplendent in papal
costume, confronts the poor little provincial gripes without any juice left in him
along the dirty little Liffey, "the boggylooking stream" (153.03) of his "Dubville
brooder-in-low" (153.18). Yet within this Hibernian, localized power struggle,
the avatar of all Irish nationalist troubles, the passage proceeds in easy Wakean
elisions to other examples of local identities succumbing to larger powers.
There is the perdurable presence of Rome in the parody of Macaulay, "As when
that brokenarched traveller from Nuzuland" (156.33) sees the ruins of London
but the continued existence of St. Peters; New Zealand is the Old World in the
newer East, but it also contains the native Zulus of Africa oppressed by Empire.
That continued power of the church persisting through time is associated with
a particular place in Rome, the Lateran Church, "Shineshone Lateran" (152.37).
(McHugh glosses Shineshone as Shem and Shaun, but there is also the lantern's
ironic shining without illumination, as well as a residual sense of the Native
American tribe, the Shoshone.) This was a place associated with ecclesiastical
judgment of the sort Joyce always feared. Throughout church history, various
Lateran councils condemned Photius as an excommunicant (Synod of 863);
the Monophysites (a Lateran convention as early as 649); heretics named for
their native places, such as Peter of Bruges and Arnold of Brescia (the Second
Lateran Council of AD 1139); the antipope Innocent III mentioned at 152.2 (the
Third Lateran Council of AD 1179, attended by the Irish archbishop, St. Laurence O'Toole). (The Fourth Lateran Council of 1215 finalized and authorized
the *Missale romanum* over liturgies from other places, such as the Gallican or
Occidental.)

Mentioned later in the passage is that particular heresy, which for Joyce
stood as the original, local apostasy: the schism of the Eastern Church by heretic Photius and sufficiently identified by "philoquus" (156.18) (a neologism that
also suggests a lover of something like the horse of Troy to introduce breeches
and induce collapse). In like manner, we are not surprised to find mention of
the Monophysite heresy of Arius and Sabellius in "Monophysicking" (156.13),
which sounds like a medical remedy for the illness it seeks to treat. Also present
are all the challenges to the Trinity touched on in this chapter in the phrase "the
fetter, the summe and the haul it cost" (153.33). This phrase clearly indicates
the strictures embedded in religion's Trinitarian associations: *ligare*/fetters; the
stakes of apostasy, or summe, (with glances at the status of the Son, as well as of
the *Summa*); and finally, the price to be paid for heresy, the "whole it costs," as
well as the ritual burning of heretics as in a holocaust. What obsesses Stephen
as an individual Irishman in "Proteus," his descent from his all-too-Irish "consubstantial" father, recurs here in a consistent elaboration of identity politics

with its burdens spread out throughout time and space. So by a commodius vicus of recirculating rebellion, we are back at the local issues suppressed by the Nicene Creed, with heresy as much political as religious, and with all that connects religion and politics as variations onapostasy and challenge.

Throughout the "Mookse and the Gripes" section, the interrelatedness of local identities rebelling against distant dominance recurs as a theme as crucial as the conflict between time and space. The passage contains a variety of rebellions of lesser and local identities struggling for expression that led to broad political consequences. For example, the passage begins with an introduction to "fullstoppers and semicolonials, hybreds and lubberrds" (152.16). High and low art (as well as the high and low Anglican Church) combine with the punctiliousness of grammar marks, periods, and semicolons. Native traditions are compromised by semicolonial entities and by hybridity, that mixing of blood Joyce favored in the "new Celtic race." The "lubberds" also gestures faintly at Peter Lombard, another individual marked by a place name, whose status as orthodox was confirmed by the same Lateran council attended by St. Laurence in 1179. "Lubberds" also points more immediately to the Lollards, local English followers of Wycliffe and forbears of the Reformation. Logically, Cranmer (whose liturgy Joyce assiduously cited)—the foremost English Reformer and martyr to the splits with the Protestant movement—appears in the phrase, "what a crammer" (155.10); there is also another Reformation figure, the Dutchman Arminius, hidden under a guise of conformist piety as "Amenius" (155.37). Thus those who variously rebelled from Rome—Lollards, English and Dutch Reformation Protestants, Eastern heretics, and the Irish Church—are asserted as local identities against the Rome of the variously enumerated and interchangeable Popes, including "Lio the Faultyfindith" (153.35), Leo XIII who reinstated the *Index* to frighten and find fault with writers of books.

All that connects religion and politics as local variations of apostasy and challenge might even be summed up in one phrase: the "diupetriark of the wouest" (153.27). This phrase combines the conflicts of the Church Universal that claims to be unitary and infallible and which defines everything outside its ideological dominion as heretical because native. The phrase begins with a glance at the ark and then progresses chronologically from the church's foundation to that marginalized Galilean ("thou are Peter," "hic sor a stone, and on hoc stone Seter satte hoc sate" [153.24]). It alludes to the Irish Church founded by Patrick, as well as to its later suppression. It proceeds through the dual papacy that split the Western Church between Rome and Avignon, resonating Joyce's favored position that there can be no unitary authority nor a singular orthodoxy derived from it. And it returns to the Great Schism that denied the papal supremacy of Rome in the phrase "athemyst sprinkled"—where *athemys-*

*tos* is Greek for "illegitimate" (153.28). The "petriark" or patriarch who rules in place of Roman popes and cardinals, names the "other" in the language of the East to localize that strange place where, as the boy in "The Sisters" noted, "the customs were foreign."

Centralized and authoritative power, Joyce felt, always produces the least attractive result, the worst, "wouest." The phrase ends with a loss of bearing, of location (German *wo ist?*) caused by the confusion of multiple contraries (French *est* [east] and *ouest* [west]). The persistent appeal of schism for Joyce is to find a place in the space opened up by the rupture in orthodoxy where individual acts may be performed—political acts and artistic acts. The whole enterprise of the church as a unitary power Joyce regards as merely "frishermans blague" (153.29), the ring of Peter less a stricture than a Frenchman's blague or disobedient ("fresh") man's prank. In finding the local places where individual identity can be asserted in spite of oppressive and repressive hegemonies, Joyce has found his way into the space of schism, which results in another ripping good joke. From Belvedere's Whitsuntide play which disobediently parodied authority and scripture to the *Wake*'s embrace of polyvalent sectarianism, Joyce is true to his schismatic turn.

# Notes

### Chapter 1. Joyce's Misbelief

1. On this necessary paradox that Joyce employed, Steven John Morrison remarks "the relationship between heresy and orthodoxy as a primary means of avoiding alignment with either side of the polarity of assent and dissent and of profiting from this evasion" (thesis abstract). To deny the one thing, however, is to become the other, defining oneself precisely by this counterstance. By contrast, the argument about misbelief in this study claims that Joyce chooses sides and that he comes down per contra. The dialectic space Morrison claims Joyce finds lies not in his embrace of both but rather in the embrace of schism, because there Joyce can find an opening which allows freedom. Morrison's dissertation, as yet unpublished, is noteworthy for its close analysis of currents of dissent in the Catholic Church of Joyce's youth and for its treatment of actual heresiarchs Joyce mentions; while Morrison notes the spaces opened to choice by Joyce's evasions, he does not pursue the effect for Joyce of these opened schismatic spaces on the works themselves, focusing rather on the heresies proper.

2. See the entry on "Orthodoxy," 9:330. (The *Catholic Encyclopedia* is hereafter cited as *CE*, with volume and page number given. As this work is also available online, the subject heading will also be indicated.) This work brings together several issues that allow for the measure of Joyce's schismatic resistance. Foremost, bearing the imprimatur of the Roman Church hierarchy, the *Encyclopedia* is certified to be dogma. Begun in 1905 and published serially between 1907 and 1914, its years of compilation and publication span Joyce's period of catechism and education and provide the doctrines he would have heard and resisted. The *Encyclopedia's* prefatory claim to present the work "of the foremost Catholic scholars in every part of the world," v, speaks to the church's claim to universality that Joyce found so stifling; its claim to provide "proper answers to the questions" not available hitherto in English speaks to Joyce's own stubborn use of English as his contrarian stance. Most particularly, the boast that "in all things the object of the Encyclopedia is to give the whole truth without prejudice, national, political or factional," vi, is precisely the pride of asserting ultimate power and knowledge that Joyce would neither believe nor accept and which he would challenge at each point with his studied misbelief.

3. Deharbe Catechism, 144. As a measure of the doctrine taught to Joyce and all Catholics in the late nineteenth century, several catechisms in addition to the Deharbe (1912) will be cited in this study: the Maynooth Catechism of the Council of Trent (1829; see Donovan) and the Butler (1887).

4. The *Catholic Encyclopedia* notes that "it is clear that the Vatican Council introduced no new doctrine when it defined the infallibility of the pope, but merely re-

asserted what had been implicitly admitted and acted upon from the beginning and had even been explicitly proclaimed and in equivalent terms by more than one of the early ecumenical councils." See "Infallibility," 7:798.

5. See *The Emergence of the Catholic Tradition*, 1:4.

6. Pelikan notes that "the most important heresies of the early church were those that have been grouped under the name [Gnosticism]," 1:81.

7. *My Brother's Keeper*, 108.

8. Ellmann, *James Joyce* 435.

9. Ibid., 565.

10. Ibid., 596.

### Chapter 2. "A Ripping Good Joke": The Attractions of Schism

1. Fargnoli notes in *Catholic Moments* that for the play to be "performed in the chapel . . . the Blessed Sacrament had to be removed from the tabernacle" and that such a removal "becomes emblematic of the role of art in Joyce's aesthetics," 5.

2. Butler's Catechism notes that the faithful are "Obliged in conscience and justice to the support of . . . pastors," 42, and not to so oblige entails pain and sin, adducing as support the quotation from Matthew 18.

3. Compare Burrus, 357, on orthodoxy and heresy as "simultaneously revealed and reveiled through . . . textuality."

4. On the figure of Newman in Joyce, see Schwarze, 52–56. Schwarze's insightful reading of Stephen's (and Joyce's) resistance to church hegemony finds its dynamic first in Romantic freedom and then in realistic accuracy. My argument is that Joyce's resistance, while it certainly includes the elements Schwarze notes, is located within the very structures of orthodoxy by a rupture from it.

5. *My Brother's Keeper*, 68; see also Kevin Sullivan, *Joyce Among the Jesuits*, 89.

6. Ellmann, *James Joyce*, 546.

7. Different critical approaches acknowledge this combination—the terrestrial, spiritual, and aesthetic elements that coalesce in the epiphany. Fargnoli notes that in "Catholic theology the word . . . suggests a manifestation of a hidden message to the benefit of others, that is, for their salvation," 6. Morris Beja, in his authoritative *Epiphany in the Modern Novel*, remarks that Joyce "took a theological word and applied it to a literary tradition [and] by this clever device he was able to make use of its suggestive spiritual meaning and connotations . . . while . . . he avoided the necessity of overthrowing any previous literary contexts," 71.

8. *My Brother's Keeper*, 124.

9. *The Workshop of Daedalus*, 3. (The epiphany numbers cited are those given by Scholes in this edition).

10. *My Brother's Keeper*, 124.

11. Scholes and Kain, *Workshop*, 12.

12. Sullivan, 124.

13. Ellmann, *James Joyce*, 23

14. See Attwater, *Penguin Dictionary of the Saints*, 222.

15. For a discussion of Joyce's medievalism, see, for example, Umberto Eco, *The Aesthetics of Chasms: The Middle Ages of James Joyce.*

16. See Pelikan, 1:23: "According to Irenaeus, 'all heresies are derived from Simon of Samaria' . . . Eusebius himself termed Simon 'the prime author of every kind of heresy.'" Joyce would have savored the use of "author."

17. Pelikan notes "the pedigree of heresy [in] the pre-Christian and extra-Christian history of Gnosticism," 1:7.

18. Restuccia argues that Joyce "located the father's law writ large in particular in the Church," 16, and notes that the "punitive nature of the Church seems to have infected the general atmosphere" of the stories, 9. "It was the . . . genuinely potent religious Fathers—generators of patriarchal law/knowledge/vision, abusers of patriarchal power— who provoked Joyce into a lifetime of writing," 16.

19. Obviously, a work such as MacCabe's *Revolution of the Word* makes such claims: "Joyce's writing produces a change in the relations between reader and text, a change which has profound revolutionary implications," 1.

## Chapter 3. "Epicleti": The Artistic Possibilities of Schism

1. For a discussion of what he calls "vivisection," see Aubert's *Aesthetics of James Joyce,* especially 26–27.

2. See the Garland edition of *Dubliners,* Hans Walter Gabler, ed., 3n5.

3. In a very thorough critique of Joyce's misapplied Greek (various words in various works), Steppe maintains that "epicleti" has been misread and consequently overvalued as a critical term. He carefully traces mistransmission of the term through Gilbert and Ellmann but, focusing on archival evidence such as Joyce's handwriting and the critical reception of his works, neglects to account for what transgressive meaning the word might convey.

4. Ellmann's obiter dicta reads, "The word epicleti, an error for *epicleses* (Latin) or *epicleseis* (Greek)," *James Joyce,* 163. In discussing Ellmann's analysis, Fargnoli maintains that by epiclesis "Joyce clearly meant transubstantiation and not a prayer or invocation," 12.

5. *Dubliners,* Viking Critical Library edition, Scholes and Litz, eds., 255.

6. R. J. Schork, in his "James Joyce and the Eastern Orthodox Church," remarks on Joyce's attendance "throughout his life . . . at various ecclesiastical venues," 108. Schork discusses Joyce's "sporadic interest in the Greek Orthodox Church, 107, and notes that Joyce was "ecumenically irreverent [in] his fictional manipulation of Christian dogma, organization, and tradition," 109. Schork goes into great detail, perceptively offering many phrases from the *Wake* that pertain to Eastern Orthodox dogma and religious and organizational terms.

7. Maynooth Catechism, J. Donovan, trans., 195, 201. Consider the Butler Catechism on the elements: "Q. What is the Blessed Eucharist? A. The body and blood, soul and divinity of Jesus Christ, under the appearance of bread and wine"; on the Institution: "Q. Are we assured Christ changed the bread and wine into his body and blood? A. Yes by the very words which Christ himself said" at the Institution, 47, 48.

8. Jungmann, 201 (emphasis added).

9. The Latin Mass or *Missale romanum* was authorized over competing liturgies and made uniform by the Fourth Lateran Council in 1215. There are two Greek Masses, that of St. John Chrysostom, a figure who graces Stephen's thinking in the opening pages of *Ulysses* when Mulligan opens his mouth, and of St. Basil, the latter used in penitential seasons.

10. The Latin uses three perfects: "accepit . . . , fregit, deditque..." ; the Greek of both Chrysostom and Basil, a participle, "taking " λαβών, and two aorists, "broke" κλάσας and "gave" ἔδωκε.

11. See Allen and Greenough, section 290, on the participle form: "Participles denote time as present, past, or future with respect to the time of the verb in their clause"; like the Greek present versus the aorist, the Latin present participle can indicate an "attempted action" or it may indicate "an action continued in the present but begun in the past," 290a1. Also consider Woodcock's *New Latin Syntax*: "Latin participles are only three in number: present active . . . 'doing,' perfect passive . . . , and future active," section 290; further, "the present participle . . . when use[d] predicatively regularly expresses incomplete action contemporaneous with that of the finite verb. Occasionally, it is used to express long-continued . . . action," section 102.

12. Thomas Connolly notes that Joyce had two copies of the Book of Common Prayer in his Paris library, one in English (item 27) and one in French (item 185). Both will be pertinent when we examine Joyce's use of the prayer book in the *Wake*. Neither Ellmann (*The Consciousness of James Joyce*) nor Gillespie notes that Joyce had a copy in Trieste or Zurich. It will become evident from a discussion of a direct reference and an allusion in *Hero* that Joyce would certainly have seen the prayer book long before his exile in Europe.

13. Gillespie notes that Joyce in Trieste might have obtained "information on Protestant Beliefs . . . through texts like the *First Catechism*, published by the Christian Literature Society of India," 68; there is reason to believe he would have had even earlier familiarity with the religious other.

14. Marion Hatchett explains that while the original version of Cranmer's Eucharist in the 1549 prayer book did have an epiclesis based on the Greek rite, subsequent versions omitted it. This omission carried over to the 1662 book, the basis of subsequent prayer books such as the one with which Joyce was familiar. Through a convoluted history, which includes "Some Anglicans [who] had come to have high regard for Eastern Liturgies," 358, the form of an epiclesis was introduced into the Scottish rite in 1637 and again in 1764.

The only observation one can make about this history is that Joyce—had he known the epiclesis was part of the splintered past of the Anglican Church—would have found congenial such an appeal to a local and differing interpretation—both institutional and national—within Anglicanism itself; he would have seen it as replicating his own challenges to the unity of Rome. On the matter of the tenses of the Institution, Cranmer's versions are the same as those in the Book of Common Prayer, from 1662 through the years of Joyce's Catholic education and the Church of Ireland prayer book. The Oxford University Press *Book of Common Prayer* (1899) will hereafter be cited as *BCP*.

15. Cranmer's source was the missal of Salisbury, the Sarum Rite, which he mixed with Gallican rites (those suppressed by the Lateran Council to favor the Roman) and with the Eastern liturgies of his interest (Hatchett 356). Cranmer's effort to bypass Rome's authority in the *Missale romanum* is a move that previews Joyce's schismatic misdirection and rupture.

16. Hereafter cited as *NED*.

17. For brief account of these positions among the Reformation thinkers represented by the Marburg Colloquy of 1529, see Lindsay, 352–59; among the differences in positions taken on the Eucharist was the claim—maintained by Zwingli and consonant with his belief in the Host as a resemblance—that the Mass was a commemoration, a point of Protestant theology to which we will return below. Lortz notes that the Colloquy, called by the Elector of Saxony, was meant to resolve "the religious and ecclesiastical schism within Protestantism, that had been developing for a long time," 2:51; that the colloquy was caused by internal rupture among Protestants would certainly have appealed to Joyce.

18. *My Brother's Keeper*, 103.

19. *My Brother's Keeper*, 103–4.

20. *Dubliners*, Viking Critical Library edition, Scholes and Litz, eds., 255–56.

21. *James Joyce*, 66.

22. In "The Priesthoods of Stephen and Buck," Fargnoli notes the association with alchemy, 3, and goes on to cite Robert Boyle, SJ, on the theological peculiarity of Joyce's use of the term "transmute," 40.

23. In *The Years of Bloom*, 56–62, John McCourt discusses Joyce's awareness of the Greek rite; he stresses the alien and transgressive aspects, if not the consequences, of these qualities.

24. The Butler Catechism notes "the body and blood of Christ, which are *really* present under the appearance of bread and wine," 49, the added emphasis making clear the point at issue. The Maynooth Catechism is even more assertive: "Christ, whole and entire, is contained in either species." See J. Donovan, trans., 206. The Deharbe Catechism is more conciliatory: it is said to harm "the appearances only" of the wine, not the Divine Blood, 264. The *accident* itself challenges what Flynn believes.

25. *NED*, definition 4.

26. Interestingly, the Deharbe Catechism's stance on papal infallibility sounds very much as circular and self-satisfied as Mr. Power's stance in the story: "Why cannot the Pope teach error when he speaks 'ex cathedra'? Because God will not allow him to do so," 146.

## Chapter 4. The Literary Advantages of Protestantism

1. Cranmer, the collect for Second Advent; see Barbee and Zahl, *Collects of Thomas Cranmer*, 5.

2. *My Brother's Keeper*, 101. Additionally, Stanislaus notes that in the Royal Terrace residence there was a cheap edition of the Gospels, owned "by the former tenants [who] were Protestant," 100.

3. *My Brother's Keeper*, 101.

4. The tension between Joyce and authority in his texts is fruitfully examined in Mahaffey's *Reauthorizing Joyce*. She explains how Joyce "splinters the power of . . . and transformed a totalizing 'authority' into a montage of 'minorities,'" noting his "passionate resistance to . . . the authority of church [and] state," xiii.

5. Marsh notes that one million copies of the Bible were printed in 1860 alone (chapter 5, n102), even after years of significant publication numbers.

6. See Scholes, *The Cornell Joyce Collection*, 6.

7. Costello, 162.

8. Item 9 in the Cornell Collection, Division of Rare and Manuscript Collections, Carl A. Kroch Library, Ithaca, New York.

9. Despite Stanislaus' claims, Moseley argues that "Joyce's early training acquainted him with the Bible by means of the Douay and the Latin Vulgate, especially as they were made known to him through a continual hearing and reading of the *Daily Missal*," vii; much of the evidence cited below will suggest otherwise.

10. Moseley, viii.

11. Moseley discusses *Portrait* in her chapter 4 and *Ulysses* in her chapter 7.

12. Sandeen, *The Roots of Fundamentalism*, 108.

13. Yeats' esoteric and eclectic beliefs were subject to a tension of orthodoxy and apostasy much as Joyce's more traditional ones were. In his *The Mystery Religion of W.B. Yeats*, Graham Hough makes the claim that Yeats' view was "not [of] the Christian theological tradition, authorized by councils and blessed by the practice of the Church; it is a rival concern, but one which [began] to make a similar claim to authority and centrality," 7. In his biography of Yeats, when discussing the numerous spats and conflicts within the Golden Dawn, Jeffares remarks that the members within the society spoke of "schism," 124.

14. *Workshop*, 264.

15. Fleischmann, 90, 100, 91.

16. Ellmann, *James Joyce*, 67.

17. Sullivan suggests the unnamed author of the essay was Hugh Kennedy, 211, later to be—unsurprisingly—a judge.

18. Qtd. in Sullivan, 211.

19. Qtd. in Sullivan, 211.

20. *James Joyce*, 58.

21. Ibid., 140.

22. *My Brother's Keeper*, 68.

23. Sullivan suggests that, due to their "various official connections, a friendly, even familiar relationship seems to have existed between" them, 88.

24. See Schwarze, 53: "Stephen's absorption of Newman has less to do with his Catholicism than it does with Newman's personal history of ostracism and dissent."

25. On this exchange and the issue of the *Index*'s intended and failed effects on propriety in literature, see Gottfried "The Audience for Joyce's Autobiographies," where I note that Ibsen would never have come under the constraint of Rome.

26. Kearns, 47, 44.

27. Inglis, citing Alexander Humphreys, *New Dublin*, 32.

28. For an earlier placement of the process of the Catholic Church's repression of Irish sexuality, see S. J. Connolly, *Priests and People*, 204–7.

29. Although he pursues his point to ends different than those discussed here, Richard Brown argues for Joyce's liberating views of sexuality; he discusses the effect of the marriage service in defining the expectations of the institution and remarks on Joyce's familiarity with the Anglican Prayer Book, noting the copy in his Paris library, 12.

30. *BCP*, 288. See n14 to chapter 3 above.

31. In the earlier prayer book of 1549, Cranmer is even more overt about the woman's role in marriage; he has the woman pledge to be "bonere and buxum in bedde and at the borde" (*The First and Second Prayerbooks of Edward VI*). While it is unlikely that Joyce knew anything about the earlier prayer book (subsequently revised and superseded), he would have recognized and welcomed the openness that was in it.

32. *Structure and Motif*, 234.

33. In *Books at the Wake*, Atherton notes that both liturgies are used, but he does not remark what the effect of this entails, 184.

34. Ellmann remarks: "In the *Wake*, Joyce seems more relaxed about the Church and about rebellion. . . . In terms of universal history, which the *Wake* presents, the Church's *punctilio* about forgotten issues adds to the joyful polyphony." See "Perspectives," 130–31.

35. *Structure and Motif*, 237.

36. Ellmann, *James Joyce*, 596.

37. These allusions have been noted by Hart (211, 243), and Atherton (184), but not with a recognition of what it means for Joyce to have cited an English Protestant text and what schismatic elements such as power, license, and sexuality he wished to stress by so doing.

38. *Structure and Motif*, 216.

39. "Technique in *Finnegans Wake*" in Bowen and Carens, 666.

40. Ibid., 673.

41. Atherton notes that Joyce had a French translation of the *BCP*, 184; Thomas Connolly marks it as item 185.

42. *James Joyce*, 556.

43. See Ellmann, *The Conscience of James Joyce*, 101; also Gillespie, 101. Thomas Connolly does not list any Bible in Joyce's Paris library.

44. 172; Atherton fails to consider what it would mean for Joyce as a rebellious Catholic to use the Anglican text.

45. Of the question of writing and audience, Kiberd notes, "The Irish writer has always been confronted with a choice," 136; choice, it should be remembered, is the root of heresy.

46. Foster, 522, 534.

47. This claim is made so frequently without attribution that is has become a commonplace; see, for example, McGrath, *In the Beginning*: "The King James Bible played no small part in the shaping of English literary nationalism," 1; "nineteenth-century writers

and literary critics acclaimed it as the 'noblest monument of English prose,'" 1, (no attribution); the Bible "became part of the everyday world of generations of English-speaking peoples spread across the world," 3.

### Chapter 5. Schism as Politics

1. *Joyce and Politics*, 101.

2. Ibid., 100.

3. Pertinent to our discussion, Pelikan notes that the importance of the doctrine of the Trinity is "one of the reasons for the contrast between the more corporate emphasis . . . and the more individualistic emphasis" dogma presented to heretics, 1:224.

4. For a discussion of the chilling effects of the *Index* on a variety of works in the public sphere, see Herr, 37–40; for a discussion of Joyce's treatment of the *Index* within *Stephen Hero*, see "The Audience for Joyce's Autobiographies" in Gottfried, 67–71.

5. Herr discusses the church's support of capitalism against socialism and revolution, 232–36; for a different view of the church's engagement with both socialism and capitalism, see Gottfried's "Church as Industry."

6. According to the *Catholic Encyclopedia*, the moral relativism erected within "the groundwork of Modernism" was considered by the church to be influenced by Kant, by whose general agnosticism "is meant the philosophy that denies that reason, used at any rate in a speculative and theoretical way, can gain true knowledge of suprasensible things," 10:418. Morrison notes that the church had an "ability to proclaim everything at odds with its own teachings as absolutely false with regard to almost every area of human activity," thus passing beyond the bounds of the truly theological, 27; it saw in "Modernism's historical work in Scripture and theology a major threat," 28.

7. Pelikan, 5:299.

8. Pelikan underscores this same combination, although with different emphasis: "While the East–West schism stemmed largely from political and ecclesiastical discord, this discord also reflected basic theological differences," 2:170.

9. Emer Nolan notes that "Joyce's unflinching localism . . . subverts the . . . integrative, falsifying vision of cultural nationalism," 29, although he would not argue that a schismatic interest greatly helps Joyce to achieve that end.

10. Morrison remarks that Joyce was more interested in "the heresiarch himself than in the heresy he expounded," 18, although the points of the heresies always resonate with the stated concerns of a character like Stephen.

11. Of the Trinitarian debates, Pelikan pertinently remarks: "Doctrine often seemed to be the victim—or the product—of church politics and of conflicts of personality," 1:173.

12. By contrast, Seamus Deane argues in *Celtic Revivals* that Joyce's "real disaffection with politics, Irish or international, enhanced his sense of isolation and was translated into his creed of artistic freedom," 92. However, Deane also remarks, more in concert with our discussion here, that in rebelliousness, unlike the European model, "instead of Napoleon or Beethoven . . . , Joyce chooses God the Father or Shakespeare, Sabellius or Arius . . . as the figures against which his hero defines his relationship to all that surrounds him . . . ," and that "it is fundamentally English culture . . . which is being parodied, even though the context is an Irish and European Catholic one," 83.

13. Of the details in the essay, Morrison notes that "most of the inaccuracies of Joyce's catalogue involve the issue of nationality," 161, and he provides greater analysis of the heresies.

14. According to Kevin Barry, *OCPW*, 314, "Joyce confuses John Scotus Erigena (*fl.* 850), Irish philosopher at the court of Charles the Bold, celebrated commentator on the writings of Dionysius the pseudo-Areopagite, with this John Duns Scotus, who was 'regent' of Paris University."

15. As a general description of dialectic in the passage, the commentary of Patrick McCarthy serves well. See "Structures and Meaning of *Finnegans Wake*," in Bowen and Carens, 600.

16. See "Saints and Sages," *CW*, 169, where Joyce touches on the differences between the Roman and Irish churches.

# Bibliography

## Works of James Joyce

*Critical Writings*. Edited by Ellsworth Mason and Richard Ellmann. New York: Viking, 1959. (*CW*)

*Dubliners*. 1914. New York: Viking, 1965. (*D*)

*Finnegans Wake*. 1939. New York: Viking, 1966. (*FW*)

*Letters*. 3 vols. Vol. 1 edited by Stuart Gilbert; vols. 2 and 3 edited by Richard Ellmann. New York: Viking, 1957; reissued with corrections, 1966.

*Occasional, Critical, and Political Writing*. Edited by Kevin Barry. Oxford: Oxford University Press, 2000. (*OCPW*)

*A Portrait of the Artist as a Young Man*. 1916. Edited by Chester Anderson. New York: Viking, 1977. (*P*)

*Stephen Hero*. 1907; posthumously published 1944. Edited by Theodore Spencer. New York: New Directions, 1963. (*SH*)

*Ulysses*. 1922. Edited by Hans Walter Gabler. New York: Random House, 1986. (*U*)

## Works Consulted

Allen, Joseph Henry, and James B. Greenough. *Latin Grammar*. London: Gin, 1888.

Atherton, James. *The Books at the Wake*. London: Faber and Faber, 1969.

Attwater, Donald. *Penguin Dictionary of the Saints*. Baltimore: Penguin, 1965.

Aubert, Jacques. *The Aesthetics of James Joyce*. Baltimore: Johns Hopkins Press, 1992.

Balsamo, Gian. *Joyce's Messianism*. Columbia: University of South Carolina Press, 2004.

Barbee, C. Frederick, and Paul F.M. Zahl, eds. *The Collects of Thomas Cranmer*. Grand Rapids: Wm. B. Eerdmans: 1999

Beja, Morris. *Epiphany in the Modern Novel*. Seattle: University of Washington Press, 1971.

*Book of Common Prayer*. Oxford: Oxford University Press, n.d., ca. 1899.

Bowen, Zack, and James F. Carens. *A Companion to Joyce Studies*. Westport, Conn.: Greenwood Press, 1984.

Boyle, Robert. "The Priesthoods of Stephen and Buck." In *Approaches to Ulysses*, edited by Thomas Staley and Bernard Benstock, 29–60. Pittsburgh: University of Pittsburgh Press, 1970.

Brook, Stella. *The Language of the Book of Common Prayer*. New York: Oxford University Press, 1965.

Brown, Richard. *James Joyce and Sexuality*. Cambridge: Cambridge University Press, 1985.

Burrus, Virginia. "Orthodoxy, Subjectivity and Institutionalization." In *Orthodoxie, Christianisme, Histoire*, edited by Susanna Elm, Eric Rebillard, and Antonella Romano, 356–60. Rome: Ecole Francaise de Rome, 2000.

Butler, James. *The Most Reverend Doctor James Butler's Catechism, revised, enlarged, improved, and recommended by the Four R.C. Bishops of Ireland*. New York: P. J. Kennedy, 1887.

*Catholic Encyclopedia: An International Work of Reference on the Constitution, Doctrine, Discipline, and History of the Catholic Church*. New York: Appleton, 1907–1912.

Connolly, S. J. *Priests and People in Pre-Famine Ireland, 1780–1845*. Dublin: Four Courts Press, 2001.

Connolly, Thomas E., *James Joyce's Books, Portraits, Manuscripts, Notebooks, Typescripts, Page Proofs*. Lewiston, N.Y.: Edwin Mellen Press, 1997.

Costello, Peter. *James Joyce: The Years of Growth*. New York: Pantheon Books, 1992.

Deane, Seamus. *Celtic Revivals*. London: Faber and Faber, 1985.

Deharbe, Joseph. *A Complete Catechism of the Catholic Religion*. Translated by John Fander. New York: Schwartz, Kirwin, and Fauss, 1912.

*Divine Liturgy of our Father Saint Basil*. (Greek and English texts.) Brookline, Mass.: Holy Cross Orthodox Press, 1988.

*Divine Liturgy of St. John Chrysostom*. 3rd ed. (Greek text with a rendering in English.) London: Faith Press, n.d.

Dix, Gregory. *The Shape of the Liturgy*. Westminster: Dacre Press, 1945.

Donovan, J., trans. *Catechism of the Council of Trent* [Maynooth]. Dublin: Duffy, 1829.

Eco, Umberto. *The Aesthetics of Chasms: The Middle Ages of James Joyce*. Cambridge, Mass.: Harvard, 1982.

Ellebracht, Mary Pierre. *Remarks on the Vocabulary of the Ancient Orations in the Missale Romanum*. Utrecht: Dekker and Van de Vegt, 1966.

Ellmann, Richard. *The Consciousness of James Joyce*. Oxford: Oxford University Press, 1977.

———. *James Joyce*. Oxford: Oxford University Press, 1982.

———. "Two Perspectives on James Joyce." In *Papers in Language and Literature*, presented to Alvan Ellegeand and Erik Frykman. Goeteborg, Sweden: Actis Universitatis, n.d.

Fargnoli, A. Nicholas. *James Joyce's Catholic Moments*. Dublin: National Library of Ireland, 2004.

*First and Second Prayerbooks of Edward VI*. London: J. M. Dent, 1910.

Fleischmann, Ruth. "Catholicism in the Culture of the New Ireland: Canon Sheehan and Daniel Cokery." In *Irish Writers and Religion*, edited by Robert Welch, 89–104. Buckinghamshire: Colin Smythe, 1992.

Fortescue, Adrian. *The Mass: A Study of the Roman Liturgy*. London: Longmans, 1912.

Foster, R. M. *Modern Ireland, 1660–1972*. London: Penguin Books, 1989.

Gabler, Hans Walter, ed., with Walter Hettche. *Dubliners*. New York: Garland, 1993.

Gillespie, Michael. *Inverted Volumes Improperly Arranged: James Joyce and his Trieste Library*. Ann Arbor: UMI Research Press, 1983.

Goodheart, Eugene. "Joyce and the Common Life." *Religion and the Arts* 1 (Spring 1997): 57–72.

Gottfried, Roy. "The Audiences for Joyce's Autobiographies." In "Joyce's Audiences," edited by John Nash, *European Joyce Studies* 14 (2002): 59-83.

———. "The Church as Industry." *James Joyce Quarterly* 41 (Fall 2003/Winter 2004): 103–10.

Griffin, Susan M. *Anti-Catholicism in Nineteenth-Century Fiction.* Cambridge: Cambridge University Press, 2004.

Hart, Clive. *Structure and Motif in Finnegans Wake.* Evanston: Northwestern University Press, 1962.

Hatchett, Marion J. *Commentary on the American Prayer Book.* San Francisco: Harper Collins, 1995.

Herr, Cheryl. *Joyce's Anatomy of Culture.* Urbana: University of Illinois Press, 1986.

Hough, Graham. *The Mystery Religion of W. B. Yeats.* Totowa, N.J.: Harvester Press, 1984.

Hynes, Sam. "The Catholicism of James Joyce." *Commonweal* 55 (February 22, 1952): 487–89.

Inglis, Tom. *Lessons in Irish Sexuality.* Dublin: University College Dublin, 1998.

Jeffares, A. Norman. *W. B. Yeats, A New Biography.* New York: Farrar, Straus, Giroux, 1989.

Joyce, Stanislaus. *My Brother's Keeper: James Joyce's Early Years.* New York: Viking Press, 1969.

Jungmann, Joseph A. *The Mass of the Roman Rite: Its Origins and Development.* New York: Benziger Brothers, 1955.

Kearns, Kevin. *Dublin Tenement Life.* Dublin: Gill and MacMillan, 1994.

Kiberd, Declan. *Inventing Ireland.* Cambridge, Mass.: Harvard University Press, 1995.

Lang, Frederic K. *Ulysses and the Irish God.* Lewisburg, Maine: Bucknell University Press, 1993.

*Lidell and Scott's Greek English Lexicon (Abridged).* Oxford: Oxford University Press, 1963.

Ligier, Louis. "The Origins of the Eucharistic Prayer: From the Last Supper to the Eucharist." *Studia Liturgica* 9 (1973): 161–85.

Lindsay, Thomas M. *A History of the Reformation.* Edinburgh: T. and T. Clark, 1906.

Lortz, Joseph. *The Reformation in Germany.* Translated by Ronald Walls. 2 vols. London: Darton, Longman, and Todd, 1940.

MacCabe, Colin. *The Revolution of the Word.* New York: Barnes and Noble, 1979.

Mahaffey, Vicki. *Reauthorizing Joyce.* Gainesville: University Press of Florida, 1995.

Manganiello, Dominic. *Joyce's Politics.* London: Routledge, 1980.

Marsh, Joe. *Word Crimes: Blasphemy, Culture, and Literature in Nineteenth-Century England.* Chicago: University of Chicago Press, 1998.

McCourt, John. *The Years of Bloom: James Joyce in Trieste, 1904–1920.* Madison: University of Wisconsin Press, 2000.

McGrath, Alister. *In the Beginning: The Story of the King James Bible and How It Changed a Nation, a Language, and a Culture.* New York: Doubleday, 2001.

Milbank, John, and Catherine Pickstock. *Truth In Aquinas.* London: Routledge, 2001.

*Missale romanum ex decreto sacrosancti Concilii tridentini restitutum s. Pii v. pontificis maximi jussu editum Clementis VIII., Urbani VIII. et Leonis XIII. Auctoritate recognitum.* Rome: Ratisbone, 1900.

Morrison, Steven John. "Heresy, Heretics and Heresiarchs in the Works of James Joyce." PhD thesis, University of London, 2000.

Moseley, Virginia. *Joyce and the Bible.* De Kalb: Northern Illinois University Press, 1967.

Mullin, Katherine. *James Joyce, Sexuality, and Social Purity.* Cambridge: Cambridge University Press, 2003.

Murray, Sir James. *A New English Dictionary on Historical Principles, Founded Mainly on the Materials Collected by the Philological Society.* Oxford: Clarendon Press, 1897.

Newsinger, John. "The Catholic Church in Nineteenth-Century Ireland." *European History Quarterly* 25 (1995): 247–67.

Nolan, Emer. *James Joyce and Nationalism.* London: Routledge, 1995.

Pelikan, Jaroslav. *The Christian Tradition: A History of the Development of Doctrine.* Vol. 1, *The Emergence of the Catholic Tradition*; vol. 2, *The Spirit of Eastern Christendom (600–1700)*; vol. 5, *Christian Doctrine and Modern Culture (since 1700)*. Chicago: University of Chicago Press, 1971, 1974, 1989.

Platt, Len. *Joyce and the Anglo-Irish.* Amsterdam: Rodopi, 1998.

Restuccia, Frances L. *Joyce and the Law of the Father.* New Haven: Yale, 1989.

Sandeen, Ernest R. *The Roots of Fundamentalism: British and American Millenarianism.* Grand Rapids: Baker House, 1978.

Schad, John. "Joycing Derrida, Churching Derrida: *Glas, église,* and *Ulysses.*" In *Writing the Bodies of Christ: The Church from Carlyle to Derrida,* edited by John Schad, 41–56. Aldershot, England: Ashgate, 2001.

Schlossman, Beryl. *Joyce's Catholic Comedy of Language.* Madison: University of Wisconsin Press, 1985.

Scholes, Robert. *The Cornell Joyce Collection.* Ithaca: Cornell University Press, 1961.

Scholes, Robert, and Robert M. Kain, eds. *The Workshop of Daedalus.* Evanston: Northwestern University Press, 1965.

Scholes, Robert, and Walton Litz, eds. *Dubliners.* Viking Critical Library edition. New York: Penguin, 1996.

Schork, R. J. "James Joyce and the Eastern Orthodox Church." *Journal of Modern Greek Studies* 17 (1999): 107–24.

———. *Joyce and Hagiography.* Gainesville: University Press of Florida, 2000.

———. "'Lowman Catolick': Irish Roman Catholic Lore in James Joyce's Fiction." *Distinguished Lecture Series 1992-1993.* Boston: University of Massachusetts, 1992.

Schwarze, Tracey Teets. *Joyce and the Victorians.* Gainesville: University Press of Florida, 2002.

Steppe, Wolfhard. "The Merry Greeks (With a Farewell to *epicleti*)." *James Joyce Quarterly* 32 (Spring/Summer 1995): 597–617.

Sullivan, Kevin. *Joyce Among the Jesuits.* New York: Columbia University Press, 1958.

Thrane, James R. "Joyce's Sermon on Hell: Its Sources and Its Backgrounds." *Modern Philology* 57 (February 1960): 172–98.

Welsh, Robert, ed. *Irish Writers and Religion.* Buckinghamshire: Colin Smythe, 1992.

Woodcock, Eric Charles. *A New Latin Syntax.* Cambridge, Mass.: Harvard, 1959.

# Index

Abbey Riots, 99–100

Adrian IV (pope), 115

Aesop, 97

Africa: marginalization of, 111

Alchemy, 49, 123n22

Allen, Joseph Henry, 122n11

Allspillouts/aspillouts, 58, 60

American Episcopal prayer book, 93–94

Anglicanism: epiclesis in history of, 122n14; marriage service in, 87–89; millenarianism as challenge to, 71–72. *See also* Book of Common Prayer; King James Bible

Anglican Mass: epiclesis in, 37–44, 50; as figuration, 47; words as representation in, 44–46

Anglicization issues, 99–101

Anticlericalism, 48

Apostasy: art as imitation of, 6–7; artistic space in, 17; attending Greek Mass as, 31–32; definition of, 4; as local and native, 115–16; as racial trait, 114; transcription as act of, 70–71, 79; visual inversion of, 68; willful adoption of, 5–6

Apostle's Creed, 102–3

Archeporoozers (phrase), 58, 59

Aristotle, 49

Arius: as church militant, 108; heresy of, 56, 57, 106–7, 109–11; local, native struggles of, 111–12, 113–14, 115

Arminius/Armenius, 117

Arnold, Matthew, 80

Arnold, Thomas, 80

Art: apocalyptic stakes of, 70; as consubstantial, 46–47; epiclesis as model for, 32; epiphany's role in, 18–21; Eucharist as analogy for, 79; Ibsen as Messiah to, 64–65; as like epicletis, 45; Mass as, 47–48; Mass as parallel to, 44; retelling of memory as, 37–38; schism as means of making, 14–16; as

similitude and as sacrament, 47–49; simony in space for, 23; thematics of possibilities in, 20–21

Ashes to ashes (phrase), 92–93

Athemystos sprinkled (phrase), 117–18

Atherton, James, 95, 125n33, 125n37, 125n41

Augustine (saint), 70, 114

Aurality, 91, 94, 97

Authorduxy: examples of, 20, 22

Authority: appropriations in break with, 20–21; of Bible, 61–62, 63, 94–95; death of fathers as break with, 24–25; disorder invited by, 5; in filiation relations, 24–25, 56–57, 103, 106–12; miscrediting of, 3–4; of narrative acts, 41; parody of, 10–11; pun as subverting, 17–18; resistance to, 6–8, 15–16, 120n4; schism as outside of, 16–17; view of Eucharist and, 25–26. *See also* Catholic doctrine; Papal infallibility; Trinity

Averroës (Ibn Rushd), 114

Babylon/babalong, 98

Barry, Kevin, 127n14

Basil (saint), 122n9

Beja, Morris, 120n7

Belief and believers: alternatives to, 1–2; imitations of, 12–13; misbelief and misbelievers compared with, 4–5, 9; visual inversion of, 68

Betrayal theme, 28–29

Bible: Catholic vs. Protestant approach to, 61–62, 63, 94–95; choice of, 26, 62–63, 67–68, 70, 95; distribution of, 63, 124n5; Greek vs. Hebrew sources of, 73; worship differences with same words from, 90–91. *See also* Biblical allusions; Douay Bible; King James Bible; Vulgate Bible

Biblical allusions: art and Revelation in, 64–66; Catholicism challenged in, 61–62, 94–95;

for understanding of, 50–55; of Trinity, 55–60. *See also* Transubstantiation

Narrative and texts: absence as presence in, 34, 60; acts of, 41; actual event vs., 32; autonomy of, 62; epiclesis as, 33–34; Greek Mass as, 35–44; heresy defined and condemned in, 13–14; Mass as remembered, 37–44; Mass as similitude and metaphor of, 44–46; model for, 21–22; schism adopted and reenacted in, 6, 25–27. *See also* Gnomon/gnostic/narrative

Nationalism, 112–13. *See also* Irish nationalism

Nepogreasymost, 58

Newman, Cardinal (John Henry), 15, 77, 81–83, 111, 120n4, 124n24

Newton, Isaac, 92

Nicene Creed: allusions to, 106–7; erasures enacted in, 110–11; filioque clause of, 56, 58, 103, 105; unitary power in, 107–9, 117

Nicholas I (pope), 105

Nolan, Emer, 126n9

*Non serviam* gesture, 6, 70–71, 103

Occam, William of, 63

Oecolampadius, Johannes, 45

"Ondt and the Gracehoper" (fable), 97

Oracle, 86

Orality/oremus/orimus, 90

Orthodoxy: death of fathers as break with, 24–25; definition of, 2–5; epicleti as challenge to, 31; heterodox conflated with, 67; Joyce's self-made, 4, 20–21. *See also* Heresy/orthodoxy paradox

Otherness: in epiclesis as narrative, 33–34; of Greek Mass, 31–32, 50–52; of language, 31–32, 58; marginalization of, 111–12; possibilities in, 29–30, 84–89; traces of, 52–53; of *Wake*'s multiphony, 87–88, 93–94, 113, 118, 125n34

Oxford Movement: allusions to, 81–83; attitudes toward, 79–80; members of, 15, 26, 77, 81–82

Papal bulls, 104, 115–16

Papal infallibility: catechisms and doctrine on, 3–4, 119–20n4, 123n26; in trinity of causes of rupture, 57–58, 59

Paralysis: efficaciousness and, 53–54; etymology of, 40; memory of, 42; misconstruction of, 23, 24; mystery of, 52; possibilities of, in "parysis," 59; synonym for, 29; as theme in *Dubliners,* 28, 33

Parnell, Charles Stewart, 28, 81, 104

Parody: of authority, 10–11, 16; possibilities of, 13, 106; of Trinity, 102–4; of Whitsuntide play, 10–11, 91, 118

Parseeism, 24

Participle form, 37–38, 39, 122n11

Pater Noster, 51, 89–90

Patriarchy, 89, 103, 117–18, 121n18

Peace be with them (phrase), 90

Peace in our time (phrase), 94

Pelikan, Jaroslav: on dogma, 5; on Gnosticism, 120n6; on heresy, 121nn16–17; on Schism, 126n8; on Trinity, 126n3, 126n11

Peter (saint), 17–18

Photius (patriarch of Constantinople): appointment of, 105–6; condemned, 116; heresy of, 56, 57, 109; local, native struggles of, 111–12, 113; in Stephen's Trinity, 102, 105, 108

Pickstock, Catherine, 49

Plymouth Brothers, 72

Pneumatic/rheumatic, 34, 59–60

Pneumax/thorax, 58, 59–60

Pola notebook, 6–7, 49

Politics: religion conflated with, 102–18; religion embedded with, 73–74. *See also* British Empire; Irish nationalism

*Portrait of the Artist as a Young Man, A*: art and religion in, 48–49; on belief, 1; biblical allusions in, 68–69; church and politics linked in, 103–4; as condensed *Hero,* 76; epiphany in, 19, 20; heresy theme in, 10–17, 61, 62, 106; Protestant passage in, 77–78; Protestant traces in, 25–27, 79–82; "schism" (term) used in, 14–16; symbolic father in, 23; on truth, 8; Vulgate Canticle in, 97–98; Whitsuntide play and authority in, 10–11, 16, 81, 91; women and sexuality in, 85

Postmodernism, 49

Poststructuralism, 49

Pots/tosspots/passports, 96

Pray for us/playfulness (phrase), 90

Protestantism: appeal of, 76–101; divisions within, 15, 123n17; freedom of discourse in,

Roy Gottfried is professor of English at Vanderbilt University. He is the author of three previous books, including *Joyce's Comic Portrait* (2000) and *Joyce's Iritis and the Irritated Text: The Dis-lexic* Ulysses (1995).

The Florida James Joyce Series
Edited by Sebastian D. G. Knowles
Zack Bowen, Editor Emeritus